THE BALANCE
Procedure

LIFESUCCESS PUBLISHING, LLC
8900 E. Pinnacle Peak Road, Suite D240
Scottsdale, AZ 85255

Telephone:	800.473.7134
Fax:	480.661.1014
E-mail:	admin@lifesuccesspublishing.com
ISBN:	978-1-59930-147-1
Cover :	LifeSuccess Publishing
Layout:	Lloyd Arbour & LifeSuccess Publishing

COMPANIES, ORGANIZATIONS, INSTITUTIONS, AND
INDUSTRY PUBLICATIONS: Quantity discounts are available
on bulk purchases of this book for reselling, educational purposes,
subscription incentives, gifts, sponsorship, or fundraising. Special
books or book excerpts can also be created to fit specific needs, such as
private labeling with your logo on the cover and a message from a VIP
printed inside. For more information, please contact our Special Sales
Department at LifeSuccess Publishing.

Printed and boumd in Great Britain by Biddles Ltd, King's Lynn, Norfolk.

THE BALANCE
Procedure

7 *EASY STEPS RESTORING BALANCE, HAPPINESS, AND MAGIC IN YOUR LIFE*

DEDICATION

To my husband, Alan, to my children, Sarah and Edward, and to my Mum, Terry, to my Dad, Tom, my sister, Carmel, and my brothers, Mark, Peter, and Stephen. Thank you for your love and support and just being there when I needed you.

ACKNOWLEDGEMENTS

My biggest thank you is to my husband, Alan, whom I have known and loved since childhood. He inspired me to write this book and supported me all the way through the process.

I also wish to thank the many teachers that I have had for their influence on my life. Angie and Bing gave me my first real introduction to spiritual healing through the Divine Force, which is ongoing within Rainbow Star Healing. The first time I met Celia Weir, she inspired me to teach as she does. She has encouraged and supported me for a long time. Many thanks go to Tam and Mair Llewellyn for their training, their belief in me, and their wonderful work setting up the AAMET site for all those interested in Meridian Energy Therapies Worldwide. From Tapas Fleming, who is such a wonderfully gentle being, I learned how easy it is to be at peace with myself. Jacquie Crooks, who is also very gentle, introduced me to Meridian Energy Therapies, which gave my life a different meaning. Gary Craig developed EFT and gave it freely to the world. I thank Ann Adams for helping me to want to expand my knowledge of Meridian Energy Therapies, and Theo Gimbel taught me the importance of colour and shape. Marshall B. Rosenberg's pioneering work in nonviolent communication has made a profound impact on my work. Dr.

Madan Kataria and his wife Madhuri, the founders of Laughter Clubs Movement, taught me how to laugh for no reason. Camille Bradstreet influenced and supported me daily with the writing of this book. My thanks also go to Dr. George Goodheart, the originator of kinesiology and muscle testing.

I would like to thank the following for being pioneers: John Diamond, for his special work on the thymus, *BK: Behavioural Kinesiology – How to Activate your Thymus and Increase Your Life Energy*, and Marshall B. Rosenberg for his pioneer work in nonviolent communication, his feeling lists, and his needs and wants lists.

One of the most powerful and transformational teachings that has influenced my life is that of Abraham-Hicks teachings; I would like to thank Ester and Jerry Hicks and Abraham for the incredibility profound, yet simple and practical teachings. If you would like free information regarding The Teachings of Abraham, visit the interactive website www.abraham-hicks.com. Thank you Jane for introducing them to me.

I would also like to thank my students and clients from whom I have learned so much. The information in this book has been a gift from them to me, for which I am truly grateful. I hope that I have, to some extent, repaid them.

To everybody I have ever met in my life, I thank you. You have all been a reflection of me in that time and space.

FOREWORD

By Professor Tamlyn Llewellyn-Edwards, Ph.D., FAAMET, FRSA, FBIH,

Modern Energy Therapies have developed in the age of computers and the Internet. This is the first time "new" therapies have been developed in this way. Of course, there is nothing new in the world and all these therapies have been developed on the backs of older traditions. However, the Internet has made a difference.

9

Just what difference has the Internet made? In the past, therapies and techniques developed slowly over a long period, as information regarding them and of modifications to them spread slowly from practitioner to practitioner. Practitioners were taught along traditional lines in schools and universities. Now, new ideas spread across the world in milliseconds, carried by the Internet to a wide variety of practitioners. Similarly, modifications, improvements, and criticisms spread equally quickly. Practitioners are trained to various levels by a host of means, many of which are less restrictive than the old schools and universities.

Is this a good idea? Generally yes, as it allows much faster development of techniques, and healing Arts moves forward swiftly and is widely available to all. It is not restricted by the dead hands of older practitioners who are eager to defend their versions of healing.

There is a downside to this in that it has tended to splinter the field of energy therapy, as different exponents of these therapies injected their own variations. Amongst the modern energy therapies we have EFT, TAT, BSFF, FREEWAY, EMDR, and a host more. These therapies have many things in common, but just as many differences. This diversion weakens the movement and confuses would-be students and practitioners.

Rather than diversity, what we need is some gathering of existing knowledge into a general therapy which can be used as a unifying central core, but without denying the wider implications of other schools of therapy. Jenny Cox's 'Balance Procedure' may well prove to be the unifying procedure we need.

10

Jenny is an experienced and enthusiastic therapist, being a practitioner and a teacher of many energy therapies, and as such she is in an ideal position to develop the needed unifying core. Her 'Balance Procedure, as presented in this volume, did not develop out of nowhere, but is the distillation of her earlier work in many fields of healing and is based on the best aspects of many earlier therapies. I strongly recommend it to you as a useful way forward.

Tickhill 2007
TLLEWELLYN@AOL.COM
Author of *Heal Yourself and Others with Meridian Therapies*
And *Success Unlimited with Energy Therapy*

TABLE OF CONTENTS

INTRODUCTION

Something drew you to this book. What was it? Was it the title? Are you seeking balance and harmony in your life? Have you decided what it is that you are trying to do with your life and need some help? The good news is that you can change negative, self-defeating beliefs and habits into positive, life-affirming thoughts and actions that you will learn using this powerful, simple procedure to transform your life-energy and those around you.

Maybe you have decided to take action in creating the life you want. What is preventing you from getting what you want? Do you want to lose weight? Do you want a new career? Do you want to change your relationships? Are you fed up with the excuses that you keep giving yourself? Have you read all of the self-help books aimed at helping you get what you want out of life but are still not taking action? What are your beliefs about what you can and can't have or do? Learn to identify where they come from, how they are affecting your life-energy, and how you can easily and simply transform them into productive, positive LIFE-ENERGY.

It is my mission to share the Balance Procedure with as many people as possible to help them take charge of their own health, wealth, and happiness.

13

Using the Balance Procedure on a daily basis means that you can always choose to override unproductive habits that have previously dictated a life that is not serving you well. Daily use of the Balance Procedure will stimulate your brain for bigger and better accomplishments. You do this by asking yourself, "What do I want?" For example, "I want to be healthier."

I will show you how to restate excuses you have used for years in positive ways to help you change the way you think. For example, you may often say or think, "I can't do that because I have no time." If you want to change that thought, use the Balance Procedure with the opposite statement, "I have all the time I need." Following through with this technique will cause your future to be vastly different from the life you are leading today! You can CHOOSE a better way of life.

When you notice compulsive, negative thoughts and behaviours, which are a by-product of our ancestral need for survival, use the Balance Procedure to help you choose joyful thoughts, no matter what may be going on around you.

You can also write a daily journal, which stimulates your brain's processing system to make advanced decisions, moving you more quickly toward your goals with intention. The journal also makes you aware of any block or belief, and you can begin thinking the opposite using the Balance Procedure. I will also show you additional therapies you can use, such as art therapy; colour gives a brilliant energy.

Learn something new! You can follow The Balance Procedure when you want to learn a new skill. It will enable you to stimulate a tired brain and infuse it with vitality. Think about some things that you want. Write them down. Don't limit yourself, thinking there are things that you don't deserve. That is negative self-talk, and we'll discuss that in-depth. Say what you want, put it on paper, and think of both large and small goals and aspirations! Below are some examples.

- **I want to learn a new language.**

- **I want to learn a new therapy.**

- **I want to practice a new sport.**

Associate with happy, productive people as much as possible. Engage in some activity such as laughter yoga, a new technique that combines traditional yoga poses and breathing with laughter or anything else that will add joy to your life. Take risks. Taking risks is taking part in living a fulfilling life, and the person who risks nothing will achieve nothing. All of your goals will be accomplished easily when you're in a state of balance because your fears and anxieties are transformed into positive, productive energy. With the Balance Procedure, we do not address the symptoms of larger rooted problems. Our aim is to first ask, "What do I want? Do I believe that I can have it?" Then we aim to remove the blockages that keep us from living the life of our dreams.

15

Using The Balance Procedure, you will easily transform blocks and beliefs that are stopping you from experiencing life to the fullest. Living in the "unknown" is the only time humans are truly alive. I welcome you on this journey of balance and joy.

During the past 20 years of studying and practising complimentary and healing practices, I've learned and used many different therapies and counselling methods in order to help clients and me find relief from physical and emotional discomfort. I am a Meridian Energy advanced practitioner and trainer, an NLP practitioner, a practitioner and trainer in holistic therapies, and a Reiki master. I am also a qualified teacher and in 2005 won the National Regional New Horizons Award for my teaching in Cambridge, United Kingdom.

I am also a fellow of The Association for the Advancement of Meridian Energy Therapies (AAMET), a nonprofit organisation open to everyone, not just holistic practitioners. My membership in Toastmaster International, the leading movement devoted to making effective oral communication a worldwide reality, is a source of great joy and laughter in my life. I consider laughter an integral part in balancing the emotions, the body, and the individual — which in turn impacts the world! I've included information on practices such as laughter yoga because I feel this brings such positive emotions which, allows energy to move quickly through the chakras and meridians to restore balance. It is also fun.

16

My teaching is not limited to the educational setting. I am a motivational speaker and run workshops nationwide on various topics, including freedom from emotional eating, addictions, phobias, public speaking, limiting beliefs, and body image. I love to work with all age groups, from babies to the elderly. I have much to add via a variety of seminars for large and small business organisations, sports professionals, schools and colleges in applying simple, self-applied balancing ideas. These foster emotional balance and enable one to regain control of any situation so that solutions can be found. My teachings are appropriate for anyone looking to take charge of his or her mental, emotional, and physical well-being.

Though my seminars and workshops will include detailed information on improving one's life, health, and attitude, I am writing this book to show everyone how simple it is to magically restore balance in an instant to improve the overall quality of life. When one can be centred and balanced, then one can achieve one's wildest dreams. It is for this very reason that I developed the Balance Procedure.

1

CHAPTER ONE

Identifying What YOU Want

To be or not to be; that is the question!

– William Shakespeare

JENNY COX

Do you know what you want? Many of us haven't ever thought about what we want in life, from life, out of life, or for our lives. We usually focus on what we don't want. One doesn't want illness, poverty, or any kind of suffering, yet often that is what prevails. On the flip side, we may know what type of car we want, what clothes we'd like to have, what type of relationship we want, or what state of health we'd like to be in, but we've become so accustomed to telling ourselves we can't have what we want. Those desires are, at best, put into some vague, abstract vision for the future. A mere wish. We settle for things and tell ourselves, "This is the best I can do, have or be."

In fact, for many of us, denying our wants has been an issue of spirituality. We've been told that to feel good is bad, that to feel bad is good, that "I want" is selfish, that we need to look after everyone else first, and that wanting "things" is a character flaw. It is a teaching of many Western religions and "spiritual" paths that poverty and suffering are good. No wonder we are confused and limit ourselves in all areas of life.

18

I'd like to share with you a different reality: You *can* have the life you desire, including physical and emotional health, without drugs. Yes, without the outside stimulants and sedatives that we use to tranquilize or avoid our reality, you can be more joyous. You can have a state of peace even though a stressful or tragic event has occurred in your life. In fact, you can achieve this quickly, and through the course of this book, I will show how to put this into practice so that you have more happiness than upset in your life, *every day*.

Life is a gift. It enables us, for a brief moment in time, to be a physical part of the total plan of creation. Understanding creates the right reaction. Treat Yourself as a trinity of mind, body, and spirit. THE BALANCE PROCEDURE IS NOT SOMETHING THAT IS DONE TO YOU, RATHER IT IS

THE BALANCE PROCEDURE

A PROCESS IN WHICH YOU ACTIVELY TAKE PART TO TRANSFORM LIMITING VALUES AND BELIEFS FOR YOUR SUCCESS.

Thinking that you lack the proper background or education is a "poor excuse" for failure. Though many of today's successful people do have the benefit of education and privilege, many do not. Success is living your dream, knowing what you want, and taking appropriate action to get it.

The "whys" of how humans on Earth ended up with this prevalent mindset of "I can't, I won't, or I shouldn't have the life I desire" is irrelevant to the process of transforming your life. It would do no good to go back and point fingers at the historical figures that may have set these ideas in motion, their lack of understanding of the basic laws of nature and the universe, or even our own families and societal influences. Just let that go. The great news is that you have control of your life. It is indeed in your hands. I understand that people are confused about what they can have, what they "deserve," or what they can accomplish due to lack of education or even over-qualification. I assure you that you are capable of having what you want, and I'd like to show you how to restore yourself to the perfection that is your birthright. It will allow all of the good things to come into your life as you open yourself up to the flow of energy that creates everything. Many of these ideas may be new to you. Some may even be a little far-fetched for you at this stage of your life, but please stay with me. You chose to read this book or attend one of my seminars because you were looking for a way to improve your situation. Each point will be explained and illustrated so that you can balance your own life — mental, physical, and emotional health — *as you read along.*

Though I offer one-on-one seminars and instruction, it is not necessary to wait for someone to come along and save you. You can and will put these simple techniques into practice.

Basically what I'm presenting to you is "transformation" by learning to balance your physical and emotional reactions. This allows change to occur. Constructive transformation is a shift in awareness. When you understand that change is for the better, you are able to accomplish these changes in your life. More specifically, transformation is when freedom of thought or action is indicated or when higher impulses are substituted for lower reactions. This is what happens in the Balance Procedure, my easy-to-apply technique of balancing yourself in every situation.

What Do You Want?

Now, knowing you can have what you want, what do you want? Start by making a list of things and circumstances you desire and state them positively and in the present tense. This helps you to feel what it is like to have these things, and then they manifest more quickly. You might want to write on a piece of paper or use the worksheet at the end of this chapter, "I am so happy and grateful now that," and fill in the blanks. Write down situations or feelings that seem both within reach and far-fetched. For example, "I want inspiration, I want purpose, I want harmony, I want to understand and be understood, I want connection, I want acceptance, I want compassion, I want love, I want affection, I want self-connection, I want to learn, I want freedom, I want creativity, I want safety, security, justice, and respect, I want to be included, I want to sing in front of thousands of people, I want to write a book, I want to climb a mountain, I want to fly a plane. I want to work three days a week. I want . . . ." Whatever issues are in your mind today, find a way to phrase them as *how you'd like them to be.*

The beauty of the Balance Procedure that I have developed and that you are about to learn is that it is easy. We can start by taking small steps to see how it works. If one wants to be healthier and fit, they can first commit to it by making the choice to add more exercise to their daily routine. But they must make time for this. They can wake up just 26 minutes earlier each day to take a brisk walk. It *is that simple* – take action. Taking these small, positive steps to improve our health improves our minds and energy levels, so that we are eager to take more small steps to improve. Seeing and feeling a result is a great motivator. I assure you that if you practice the suggestions I outline in this book, you will begin to see results immediately. If you get frustrated, I even have a quick and simple remedy for restoring that *feeling* of well-being that will keep you motivated to improve your entire life.

Perhaps you want a peaceful home life. Write that down, "I want peace and harmony with my family." Avoid phrasing things in the negative. If your spouse is grouchy or unpleasant, stay away from those thoughts about his or her negative behaviours. Write down, "I want my partner to understand and respect me. I want fun and laughter with my partner. I want to be appreciated when I have cleaned or cooked a meal for my family." Focus on what is good about those around you. It is important to note that we cannot change another person, like our spouse, parent, child, or co-worker; however, we do have the power to influence. We are responsible for much of the atmosphere in our home and workplace, so if we begin to change our own attitude, thoughts, and participation in a community or environment, we'll often find that those around us respond to the positive changes. Likewise, when we react negatively to circumstances, we are continuing to create the negative atmosphere to which those around us respond.

It is common for individuals to have difficulty determining what they want. As I said earlier, we have become accustomed to thinking in terms of what we don't want or thinking that we can't have what we want. Take time to adjust your thinking. It isn't always as easy as thinking about the opposite of what you don't want. You may or may not want to drive a luxury car, but there are numerous choices if what you desire is a new car.

It can be quite fun to determine what you do want. Make the process as joyous as possible. Let's say you have a friend who has a vehicle you like. Sit in it. Feel it. Smell it. Then go to a dealership and test drive it — a brand new one. Take a test drive of all sorts of vehicles, and make a list of those you might like to have. Get pictures and put them in places where you can see them. Visualise yourself driving all sorts of vehicles until you arrive at one you like.

The same practices can be put in place for all sorts of desires. Perhaps you'd like to be a different dress or suit size. Find a picture of the ideal body, and paste your face on it or draw it out. Creating our desires from our own artistic talents is a great way to manifest what you want. Writing down, "I want to lose weight" has the same effect as writing, "I want to quit smoking." Perhaps you'd like to gain weight. Our thoughts about our physical bodies often block the appropriate flow of energy to restore optimal health.

22

Do you want more energy? What about the foods you eat and beverages you drink? Have you learned to eat for reasons other than body hunger? Have you learned to diet and control food? Have you learned to criticise and judge yourself? Do you seek self-improvement to make yourself more loveable? Have you learned to eat in order to cope with your feelings? Dealing with destructive behaviours must begin with understanding the flow of energy. Chapter Five is devoted entirely to the concept of energy and the laws governing it. The process begins with determining what you want and adjusting your thoughts to allow your desires to come into being.

Have you been diagnosed with some malady or pain affliction? Put it in the positive, "I am whole. I am healthy." Suggesting that you need to be healed indicates that you are holding onto the idea that you are broken. This is another idea I will focus on throughout the book. Contrary to many teachings regarding human nature, I contend that we are perfect at birth. It is your birthright to be healthy and happy. State your desired health in positive, affirming, present-tense terms: "I am whole. I am healthy." Visualise what it feels like to be healthy. It doesn't matter how those around you define health or if a doctor or other practitioner has told you that your symptoms are normal. What do you want to feel like? State it. Write it down. Acknowledge that you deserve this state of well-being. I will show you how to easily achieve this desired state of well-being daily, which will open you up to the restoration of health and wholeness.

Who Do You Want to Be?

As children, we are told that we can be anything we want to be. Yet, as we grow up, our concept of reality changes, often due to the influence of others. Well-meaning individuals may often seem to want to "rob us" of our dreams regarding career choice or our place in society by negating our dreams. They will make comments like, "You can't make any money doing that." The truth is you can be whoever you wish to be. Setting personal goals is healthy. We should strive to be the best at whatever we wish to do. It doesn't matter if you wish to be a postal clerk, a farmer, a prime minister, a rap artist, or a concert cellist. However, the way you earn money does not really define who you are. I do acknowledge that this issue is important to many people though. Having work that satisfies and brings meaning into your life is significant. It is often how we bring the rest of our lives into balance by providing for basic needs first and then the niceties.

23

We must also look within ourselves to see what our beliefs on ethics and integrity are. Are you living up to the moral codes and ethical behaviours that resonate with you? Let me rephrase this. Are you comfortable with your actions and thoughts on a daily basis? When we do something that is not harmonious with who we are, it affects our moods and emotions.

Let's say you are a salesperson. You know that "playing fair" is a rule in sports, but you've become accustomed to the notion that it is a "dog eat dog" world in the field and that the best salesperson is the one who closes the most deals. However, if you "steal a sale" from a co-worker, how does that really make you feel inside? Do you justify it and push the guilty emotion out of your conscious mind? Is there a part of you that feels badly about the transaction? Examine how you feel with your actions. Are you living the life of the person you wish to be?

Perhaps you complain to a co-worker or friend about your spouse. Though you love this person, he or she does something that irritates you. How does the complaining make you feel? There is a better alternative to grumbling. Recognising the positive actions of those around us will help more of those actions we love to surface. As John Grey, author of *Men are from Mars, Women are from Venus*, says, "Every man knows that when his wife is grateful for the little things he does, he wants to do more of them." This applies to both sexes and people of all ages. When we are appreciated, we want to do more of the things that make people around us happy and grateful! When people are joyful, it is contagious!

You may need some time to define what you want and who you are or want to be, but you can start immediately. Changing your desires as you grow is fine. As children, our greatest desire may have been a bicycle or roller skates. Today, it may be that new vehicle. Our desires and wants changed as we grew up. You are on a path, a journey, of growing into balance. Expect your wishes to grow along with you.

Doesn't it seem ironic that as we age we seem to run out of steam? Why are 2–year-olds blessed with the abundant energy we should have? Maybe they don't know yet that they are anything but perfect.

THE BALANCE PROCEDURE

A common complaint from people who can't seem to achieve their career or family goals is the lack of time they feel they have. They always feel rushed or exhausted. A change in mental attitude can help with the feeling of well-being, and affirmations such as "I have all the time I need" are appropriate for many individuals and families. The feeling of being rushed creates a chaotic state that disrupts a natural flow. Even if you're held up in traffic or have to make an unexpected stop, the return to balance and that state of well-being during this process will calm the nervous system and allow you to make the necessary adjustments to your schedule in order to accomplish the desired tasks. Sometimes we have to choose — or prioritise. Consider this. Are your priorities in line with who you'd like to be? Like organising our cupboards or wardrobes in order to see what is in there, organising our priorities is a way to see who we want to be versus who we are now.

This is a good place to remember that, as children, we often looked forward to surprises. The unexpected was thrilling. It was magical. Why is it that, as adults, we sometimes dread surprises? We cannot know what is to come even for one day. There are too many variables to consider. If we remain balanced and not agitated throughout the course of the day — like when we're stuck in traffic, the office copier fails, there's a sick child at home, no telephones are working, the Internet is down, and the boss is on a rampage — then the surprises that do come, those unexpected outcomes, might just be *pleasant surprises.* You'll find you rise to the occasion. But at minimum you maintain a healthy digestive system and blood pressure because you didn't let the stresses get to you.

Stress affects everything in our world, but we're in control. We control how we let stress affect us or not. It is a choice, but it is one we do have to put into practice. We first must know what it feels like to *be* balanced before we can feel it and strive for it.

What Magic Will Put Your Life in Balance?

Do you really want to change? What are you willing to do to create that change? The choice is yours. Often, when faced with ideas for improvement or initiating change, humans don't want to make the effort. But that is understandable if the goal is so lofty that it seems unreachable. If our desire is to lose 35 pounds, then facing a six-month diet and exercise program that hurts and limits the sensations that cross our taste buds is not a tempting process! But what if we break it down? What if we still want to lose the 35 pounds, but we convince ourselves that increasing exercise and foregoing dessert *just for today* is enough. If we add (and subtract) those two commitments each day, within a week we're likely to have dropped a pound, perhaps even two. Six months is roughly 24 weeks. Start with small changes. Deciding what path to follow or just explore is a great beginning. Let's add to those simple commitments the desire to maintain that feeling of well-being more often than we let ourselves lose that state. Do you "stress eat?" Perhaps you eat the equivalent of two complete meals each week because of stress. How quickly, then, can you lose those 35 pounds if you're handling stress rather than heading for the fridge when it hits you? It doesn't solve the issue. It seeks to ease the symptom. I am not discounting the need for Western medicine. It has its place; however, most common issues can be best handled by taking back control of your life and health. Understanding certain natural laws, practicing simple energy-balancing techniques, eating a proper diet, and exercising will give you that control. If the world's greatest gymnast becomes unbalanced when trying to cross a balance beam, they must first regain their balance before they can return to their routine. It all comes with practice.

The magic that will transform your life will come when you apply the ideas of this book and other positive ideas and information and surround yourself with people who know that these are truths. YOUR OLD BELIEFS WILL NO LONGER

THE BALANCE PROCEDURE

EXIST AS YOU PUT THE BALANCE PROCEDURE
INTO PRACTICE. YOU'LL FIND THEY HAVE BEEN
TRANSFORMED INTO POSITIVE AND PRODUCTIVE
THOUGHTS AND WAYS OF LIVING, AND YOUR
LIFE-ENERGY WILL BE STIMULATED. YOU
CAN NOW FACE YOUR LIFE WITHOUT BEING
OVERWHELMED BY FINANCIAL FEAR. IF THE FEAR
RETURNS FOR WHATEVER REASON, THEN DO
THE BALANCE PROCEDURE. You cannot exist in a state
of harmony, joy, and balance around people who have a fatalistic,
unhealthy, or defeated view of life. You can choose not to buy
into the negative ideas of others with whom you have contact,
but a journey of health and happiness becomes easier when you
surround yourself with others who share a similar worldview.
The very fact that you picked up this book indicates that you
are already on that journey. You will find others who share this
view because you have already taken the baby step to bring that
into your life. I'll discuss this more in Chapter Four. Energy
attracts like energy. Did your mother or father ever say to you,
"Tell me who your friends are, and I'll tell you who you are?" On
an energetic level, this is 100% true. There are even some very
interesting studies done regarding income. It has been shown that
you are probably going to earn within 10% of what your "circle of
influence" earns each year. Money is also energy, though it tends
to come in paper or electronic form. So if you desire an increase
in income, consider whom you associate with on a daily basis.
Are they driven, motivated, balanced individuals? Or are they
scattered, depressed complainers who refuse to balance even their
checkbooks?

27

We are often in a prison of our own making. Financial
insecurity is a big issue in the world. It is important to know that
money feelings are virtually never about money; they are about
relationships. Money is a symbol of energy that gathers strength
as it passes from one person to another. Money itself has no

meaning, but it can be considered a symbol of relationships. The way we deal with money is the way we deal with our relationships. Money always comes attached to people, so your fear of running out of money is really about your fear of running out of people, being left alone and not having your wants and needs met. In other words, I contend that money issues are actually emotional issues that have manifested symptoms in our physical world. I do not have the same approach to money as your financial advisor does. We probably have radically different philosophies.

Money problems and patterns can be a clue to your self-image and personal identity. For example, when people say that they don't earn enough money to support themselves, it usually means that they feel unsupported and unappreciated. People who never have enough money usually feel that they are not enough and have little to offer. A person's net worth is often a reflection of his or her self-worth. The Balance Procedure transforms these beliefs by changing the inner dialogue to, "I want to be appreciated, and I want to feel supported. I am enough!"

28

Determining what you want, who you want to be, how you intend to bring about those changes, or what tools you'll use to initiate these changes is your mission for the next few days. I'm including some very brief worksheets. You may use any template you wish. Create a collage of desired physical items, such as cars, homes, watches, or whatever you fancy.

Practice smiling instead of frowning. It may take effort, but if you try this simple act, you'll find that others smile back at you. It, too, is contagious. Hold open a door for someone today. Or retrieve a dropped object for someone before he or she stoops to get it. And smile. It is a great place to start to restore your balance by just choosing to have more moments of happiness in your day.

THE BALANCE PROCEDURE

Science has discovered that nothing can vanish without trace. Nature does not know destruction, only transformation.

– **Werner von Braun**
Rocket Scientist

What do you want? List anything and everything you can think of in the positive.

1. fill up my passport
2. ABUNDANT ENERGY
3. A BEAUTIFUL SMILE
4. LOTS OF HUGS
5. money to spend
6. A HOME IN THE COUNTRY
7. AN ORAGANIZED + CLEAN APARTMENT
8. TO SAY YES TO OPPORTUNITIES
9. TO SAY yes to myself –
10. TO BE USED AS AN INSTRUMENT OF GOD
11. To come FROM JOY
12. TO USE my creativity FOR GOOD
13. TO GET TO KNOW my SISTER

14. To live each day with purpose
15. To be in a loving relationship
16. ~~MAKE~~ Have people to do things for me
17. have security
18. be true to myself
19. meditate
20. Embrace life fully

Say yes every chance I get

21. Don't stop here if you have more, or make lists for multiple issues or themes!

Go for it // take chances

Trust in myself and the universe to give me what I need + want!

Creating people who want me to take their pictures and are happy to pay me—

CHAPTER TWO

Believe Me!

Have you ever stopped to think about the beliefs and values
that you have been taught about how your life is suppose to be?
Ask yourself: where have my beliefs originated? How do they guide
how I live my life? Do my values and beliefs serve me? Why is it so
important to understand limiting beliefs and values in any change
process?

Balance cannot be achieved when one limits the freedom
and choices of other humans, *or oneself*, regarding basic principles.
From the moment we are conceived, we begin to pick up
influences from those around us. Many of these influences have
been programmed into our subconscious minds, but by learning
to recognise these influences and the role they play in our life
dramas, we can identify and transform those influences that cause
us discomfort and block our progress. We can do this using the
Balance Procedure.

32

Many people are conditioned to feel that life has to be
hard work, drudgery, and a bore. "You don't get something for
nothing" is the underlying principle we typically hear from our
parents and relatives. Many people also believe that living and
learning through suffering, deprivation, and hard knocks is the
way to build character. They are convinced that living and learning
without a lot of strenuous effort breeds a pattern of laziness. I
believe that in transforming these influences or beliefs, far from
putting in no effort, you are really being super conscientious.
You are making the most economical use of your body's energy
resources. The body gets its energy from the food and nutrients
we consume. Nowadays most body energy is wasted on tension,
anxiety, worry, strain, and boredom; there is less energy for actual
life and learning. The Balance Procedure strives to create a link
between conscious and unconscious, thus producing a third state
of *super-consciousness*. My definition here differs from Jungian
psychology. What I mean is that we achieve a higher state of
consciousness.

Nature, like humans, is perfect. It is always in balance. It is our job as humans to work within the laws of nature. Understanding these laws can set you on a path to freedom.

Determining Limiting Decisions

So what do we do to change these limiting beliefs? First, recognise that they are not your own! Each time in the past when you adopted a limiting belief, a limiting decision preceded that acceptance. You were operating under a set of predetermined decisions. A limiting decision preceded even the beliefs that were adopted from other people. Maybe you thought, "This person is an authority; they must be right." You took on that belief without any thought or consideration of the fact that they might be wrong. If you say, "I don't believe I can do it," ask yourself when you decided that or who decided that for you.

33

Determining our limited beliefs caused by limited decisions is an important step in changing our lives to bring about balance and harmony. Once you find the initial decision, you will be able to identify those influences and transform them. You will see your body and your entire being, including your energy system and spirit, soul, or mind as part of the whole you that will be returned to balance!

Biologist Karl Ludwig von Bertalanffy developed a General System Theory. He explained to us that the whole universe is composed of systems and subsystems. Simply put, Bertalanffy's model argued for holism over reductionism. He showed that systems work as a whole, not in parts.

For example, in my own reality I have a circulatory system, nervous system, and endocrine system. All these systems are within my body, yet you could never have a relationship with me just by understanding these subsystems. Those subsystems all come together in a system called Jenny Cox.

I am also part of a family system, that is part of a cultural system, that is part of a religious system, that is part of a country system, that is part of a world system, that is part of a solar system. Each system has laws, which are part of a universal system. If you look microcosmically or macrocosmically, you will always find a system.

Laws govern systems, whether they are biological systems, solar systems, or energetic systems. Since a family is a system, laws govern families. Understand these laws from your own community system so you can understand some of the things that have impacted your life. Know the system from which you came, and you know what the dynamics were in that system. All families don't operate with the same set of laws — that's why comparisons of family units don't work!

34

Growing up you had a definable role in the family, such as the hero, the scapegoat, or perhaps the lost child. Which role were you assigned? Do you want to let it go? You can use the Balance Procedure to help you eliminate any discomfort that the process of change stimulates, including frustration with the process. The Balance Procedure will not change your behaviour; you have to be willing to change your habitual self-talk and destructive behaviours. Treat the issues that come up as you are going through this process of change while remaining open to finding the source of these issues. The Balance Procedure is a tool to transform the individual; your job is to use it.

As you recognise these limited beliefs and decisions and take steps to change them, they are transformed into positive productive energy. The Balance Procedure strives to create a link between conscious and unconscious, thus producing a third level of evolved thinking.

THE BALANCE PROCEDURE

I mentioned earlier that money always comes attached to people, so your fear of running out of money is really your fear of running out of people. When we balance our emotions and relationships, we often find that our money situations work out in ways that are better than we thought possible.

When your old beliefs have been transformed into positive and productive beliefs and your life-energy has been stimulated, then you are balanced. You can now face your life without being overwhelmed by financial fear, or any other anxiety for that matter. If the fear returns for whatever reason, do the Balance Procedure to return to centre-balance before the fear creates physical symptoms in the body.

How's your health? What is your self-talk about it? Are you a victim of your family's system of laws? Did your mum have diabetes? Is heart disease in your family? What other ailments are you, or were you, convinced you'd develop due to "family history?" If our bodies operate as a whole and the brain feeds the information to the endocrine system that women of this bloodline develop thyroid problems at age 30 based on the "family history," what do you suppose happens? Genetics may be a more complex issue, but if it were governed by laws, then we'd ALWAYS see women of a certain clan develop thyroid issues at age 30. Genetic disease doesn't work that way. Sometimes ailments develop; sometimes they don't. On the hit DVD *The Secret*, author Lisa Nichols tells us, "What we think about, we bring about." This applies to all areas of our lives and all systems. Deepak Chopra says that in quantum physics, the study of subatomic movement, scientists speculate that some systems don't even operate without thought. That is hard to digest, but as you apply the Balance Procedure and begin to change the conversations you have with yourself, you'll see how it applies to you: a system within a system.

Beliefs include things you trust to be true and what you believe you can or cannot do. Many negative and limiting beliefs are unconscious and have been influenced by parents, teachers, friends, and others. Beliefs help you make sense of the world around you. They can empower you to achieve success or limit your thinking about success.

What we communicate to ourselves is what becomes true in our lives. It has been estimated by scientists that we talk to ourselves at 300 words per minute; this can be a wonderful way to pass the time if you have something helpful and entertaining to say to yourself. Try a "self-talk experiment." Say one of these phrases out loud, "People like me for who I am. I am a lovable person. I am really clever." Then, close your eyes and listen to the voice in your head–your "self talk." Did you hear great follow-up statements? Our self-talk can have an emotion attached to it affecting how we deal with current situations.

Similar patterns surface in every area of our lives: health, wealth, or interpersonal relationships. In fact, it is probably easiest to see in relationships with other people. Have you been influenced by the same type of relationship your parents had? How are your relationships with your children and siblings? Does this reflect any of the talk or conditioning that went on in your family? Perhaps your mum, or another female member of your circle of influence made comments such as, "You can't trust men." What sort of romantic relationships did they have? If you bought into their negative talk, what sort of relationships have you created? This stereotype, we know, is unfair. All men are not untrustworthy. Human beings are products of the various systems going on within and around them. Just knowing what YOU want from a relationship is a great start. You may want appreciation, respect, or connection. This will create the relationships and true connection.

THE BALANCE PROCEDURE

In the late 1950s and 1960s, a Canadian psychologist, Albert Bandura, broke ground in the world of psychology by experimenting with behaviourism. This branch of psychology uses experimental methods and focuses on observable variables, specifically those that can be measured and manipulated. Bandura is most famous for an experiment where he had 5-year-olds watch a video of a woman beating a "Bobo doll," a blow-up plastic doll with sand weighing it at the bottom and the image of "Bobo the clown" on its front. The woman used her fists and a small hammer to hit the doll and even exclaimed "sockeroo" on occasion. The children were then irritated by being placed in a room with toys that they could not play with.

Later, the children were put in another room with the "Bobo doll," and many of the children imitated what they'd seen a grown woman do on film. Bandura referred to this as "modelling." He continued to vary his experiments until he arrived at something that he could determine to be a norm for humans. Dr. C. George Boeree, in his published paper on Bandura's work, titled simply "Albert Bandura," summarizes the complex psychological progress that Dr. Bandura's work made for us. He writes:

All these variations allowed Bandura to establish that there were certain steps involved in the modelling process:

1. **Attention.** If you are going to learn anything, you have to be paying attention. Likewise, anything that puts a damper on attention is going to decrease learning, including observational learning. If, for example, you are sleepy, groggy, drugged, sick, nervous, or "hyper," you will learn less well. Likewise, if you are being distracted by competing stimuli.

Some of the things that influence attention involve characteristics of the model. If the model is colourful and dramatic, for example, we pay more attention. If the model is attractive, or prestigious, or appears to be particularly competent, you will pay more attention. And if the model seems more like yourself, you pay more attention. These kinds of variables directed Bandura toward an examination of television and its effects on kids!

2. Retention. Second, you must be able to retain — remember — what you have paid attention to. This is where imagery and language come in: we store what we have seen the model doing in the form of mental images or verbal descriptions. When so stored, you can later "bring up" the image or description, so that you can reproduce it with your own behaviour.

3. Reproduction. At this point, you're just sitting there daydreaming. You have to translate the images or descriptions into actual behavior. So you have to have the ability to reproduce the behaviour in the first place. I can watch Olympic ice skaters all day long, yet not be able to reproduce their jumps because I can't ice skate at all! On the other hand, if I could skate, my performance would in fact improve if I watch skaters who are better than I am.

Another important tidbit about reproduction is that our ability to imitate improves with practice at the behaviours involved. And one more tidbit: Our abilities improve even when we just imagine ourselves performing! Many athletes, for example, imagine their performance in their mind's eye prior to actually performing.

38

4. Motivation. And yet, with all this, you're still not going to do anything unless you are motivated to imitate, i.e., until you have some reason for doing it. Bandura mentions a number of motives:

> **a. Past reinforcement: a la traditional behaviourism**
> **b. Promised reinforcements: incentives that we can imagine**
> **c. Vicarious reinforcement: seeing and recalling the model being reinforced**

Notice that these are, traditionally, considered to be the things that "cause" learning. Bandura is saying that they don't so much cause learning as cause us to demonstrate what we have learned. That is, he sees them as motives.

39

Of course, the negative motivations are there as well, giving you reasons not to imitate someone:

> **d. Past punishment**
> **e. Promised punishment (threats)**
> **d. Vicarious punishment**

Like most traditional behaviourists, Bandura says that punishment in whatever form does not work as well as reinforcement and, in fact, has a tendency to backfire on us.

Self-regulation

Self-regulation — controlling our own behaviour is the other "workhorse" of human personality. Here Bandura suggests three steps:

1. Self-observation. We look at ourselves, our behaviour, and keep tabs on it.

2. Judgment. We compare what we see with a standard. For example, we can compare our performance with traditional standards, such as "rules of etiquette." Or we can create arbitrary ones, like "I'll read a book a week." Or we can compete with others, or with ourselves.

3. Self-response. If you did well in comparison with your standard, you give yourself rewarding self-responses. If you did poorly, you give yourself punishing self-responses. These self-responses can range from the obvious (treating yourself to a sundae or working late) to the more covert (feelings of pride or shame).

A very important concept in psychology that can be understood well with self-regulation is self-concept (better known as self-esteem). If, over the years, you find yourself meeting your standards and [have a] life loaded with self-praise and self-reward, you will have a pleasant self-concept (high self-esteem). If, on the other hand, you find yourself forever failing to meet your standards and punishing yourself, you will have a poor self-concept (low self-esteem).

Recall that behaviourists generally view reinforcement as effective and punishment as fraught with problems. The same goes for self-punishment. Bandura sees three likely results of excessive self-punishment:

THE BALANCE PROCEDURE

a. Compensation — a superiority complex, for example, and delusions of grandeur.
b. Inactivity — apathy, boredom, depression
c. Escape — drugs and alcohol, television fantasies, or even the ultimate escape, suicide

These have some resemblance to the unhealthy personalities Adler and Horney talk about: an aggressive type, a compliant type, and an avoidant type, respectively.

Bandura's recommendations to those who suffer from poor self-concepts come straight from the three steps of self-regulation:

1. Regarding self-observation. Know thyself! Make sure you have an accurate picture of your behaviour.

2. Regarding standards. Make sure your standards aren't set too high. Don't set yourself up for failure! Standards that are too low, on the other hand, are meaningless.

3. Regarding self-response. Use self-rewards, not self-punishments. Celebrate your victories; don't dwell on your failures.

(http://webspace.ship.edu/cgboer/bandura.html)

This study, which is published in several of his books but which appeared in his first work *Adolescent Aggression* in 1959, led to the belief that television was responsible for a rise in violent crimes in American society. Critics of this study have claimed that if this is so, then there is another side of this argument. Joyful, pleasant images on television should lead to joyful and pleasant behaviour.

In any case, most of us do accept that the images, behaviours, sounds, and scents we surround ourselves with will affect our mood. We change the music to suit our mood or even to change our mood if we are aware of this tendency.

Let's look at our relationships with children. In 1979, the rock group Pink Floyd had a hit song *Another Brick in the Wall* with the lyrics, "We don't need no education; we don't need no thought control." The theme of this song was negative and showed quite well just how negative influences and comments from educators affected the children they taught. Young people could relate to the constant verbal abuse from authority figures, and it created a following of individuals who rejected formal education because of its tendency to be negative. It was an angry song that stirred up angry emotions and reactions.

What is really sad is that any learning that's been motivated by coercion often produces negative effects. Coercion tactics are identifiable when a student who is learning anything is doing so out of fear of punishment, out of a desire for rewards in the form of grades, to escape shame or guilt, or out of a sense of "should," "must," or "ought." Learning is too precious to be motivated by any of these coercive tactics. Let's remember what Bandura deduced in the 1950s, "punishment in whatever form does not work as well as reinforcement and, in fact, has a tendency to 'backfire' on us."

Learning that's motivated by love for life and by a desire to learn new skills that help us to better create, evolve, and expand for our own and others' well-being is what leads to positive self-talk and healthy self-esteem.

We have the choice of losing who we think we are and finding ourselves beyond the influences that have created our being. We have the choice of being stuck with our fixed view of life or of changing it. Our task is to take responsibility for our own learning and evolution. Nothing is permanent; nothing is fixed. We can reach far beyond our limiting beliefs. The universe is constantly expanding, so our journey is about expansion of our reality and our lives. Our potential in life is limitless, and the choice is ours. As long as there is life, our potential can be realized. The ultimate choice is up to life, and we are that life.

> *Regarding self-response, use self-rewards, not self-punishments. Celebrate your victories; don't dwell on your failures.*
>
> **– Dr. C. George Boeree
> on the work of Dr. Albert Bandura**

How Do You Feel? 43

Unless feelings are aroused to an intense level, it may be difficult to answer this question. Feelings occur in the brain and several other parts of the body at the same time. They take place when stimulated by something either internal or external.

Emotions are the outward expressions of our feelings. Anger, fear, love, and grief are four of the most basic feelings that every human has in common. Other names we give to feelings are variations of these four.

Become More Aware of How You Feel.

Throughout the week, stop every now and then to consider how you feel. Notice where you feel any sensations, aches, movements, or changes in temperature. You may discover that different feelings give the same sensations. Some feelings may never seem to get to the surface, but leave you aching and sick instead. These are usually blocked feelings.

Do you express an emotion that is opposite to what you really feel, such as getting angry when you feel like crying? Do you avoid finding out what you feel? Are you suppressing your feelings? Completing your feeling diary will help you to become more aware of your feelings.

Complete Your Feeling Diary.

Over a week, make a note each day of which feelings you were aware of experiencing that day by checking the names of the feelings on the list. If you can identify when you have an emotion, consider where you feel it in the body. Emotions are the body's physical, visceral response to the vibrational state of being caused by whatever you are giving your attention to.

Are Your Feelings Natural or Acquired?

When you have completed your diary, you may like to consider whether or not one of your parents might have produced a similar feeling diary.

The table on the next page are feelings that we all have. To observe these feelings, we can start to identify universal needs that may not be met. After you have filled in the week's diary, check the needs table that was inspired by Marshall B. Rosenberg, author of *Nonviolet Communication*. By observing how we feel we can easily identify needs that are not being met. We then take responsibility of how we feel and put our intention out there for

THE BALANCE PROCEDURE

the need to be fulfilled. Example: I am confused my need would be to understand and be understood, later you will be able to do the balance procedure with all your basic needs that are universal to every human being on the planet. When we are feeling joyful, amazed, confident, stimulated, optimistic, inspired, thankful, energetic, relieved, comfortable, our basic needs are being fulfilled. The diary below is when our basic needs are not fulfilled.

My feeling diary for the week...							
	T	F	S	S	M	T	W
Angry							
Afraid							
Disconnected							
Bored							
Vulnerable							
Hopeless							
Lonely							
Nervous							
Annoyed							
Concerned							
Impatient							
Depressed							
Optimistic							
Uncomfortable							
Impatient							

	T	F	S	S	M	T	W
Overwhelmed							
Helpless							
Tense							
Sad							

Some Basic Needs We All Have, Inspired by Marshall B Rosenberg, Author of *Nonviolent Communication*:

CONNECTION

Acceptance

Affection

Appreciation

Belonging

Closeness

Communication

Community

Cooperation

Companionship

Compassion

Consideration

Consistency

Empathy

Inclusion

Intimacy

Love

Mutuality

Nurturing

Respect/Self-respect

Safety

Security

Stability

Support

To know and be known

To see and be seen

To understand and be understood

Trust

Warmth

HONESTY

Authenticity

Humour

Integrity

Joy

Play

Presence

PEACE

Beauty

Communion

Ease

Equality

Harmony

Inspiration

Order

PHYSICAL WELL-BEING

Air

Food

Movement/Exercise

Rest/Sleep

Safety

Sexual Expression

Shelter

Touch

Water

MEANING

Awareness

Celebration of life

Challenge

Clarity

Competence

Consciousness

Contribution

Creativity

Discovery

Effectiveness

Efficacy

Growth

Hope

Learning

Mourning

Participation

Purpose

Self-expression

Stimulation

To matter

Understanding

49

AUTONOMY

Choice

Freedom

Independence

Space

Spontaneity

- Needs are the resources required for you to sustain and enrich your life.

- Needs are universal; everyone has needs.

- Needs make no reference to any specific person doing any specific thing

50

The first step in the Balance Procedure is identifying what your needs are. Your feelings are your guidance to giving you an internal message if your needs are being met or not. Using the Balance Procedure, we are able to identify the stimulus for our feelings without confusing it with an evaluation or judgement toward ourselves or others. We can bring our full intention to our needs, and can transform negative energy into positive productive energy.

Identify How You Feel.

1. Identify how I feel.

    What do I need?

2. Identify how I feel.

    What do I need?

3. Identify how I feel.

    What do I need?

4. Identify how I feel.

    What do I need?

5. Identify how I feel.

    What do I need?

6. Identify how I feel.

    What do I need?

7. Identify how I feel.

    What do I need?

3

CHAPTER THREE

An Introduction to
Western Medicine and
Eastern Philosophy

Understanding that there is a fundamental difference in the evolution of Eastern and Western medical traditions and philosophy is necessary for understanding why the Balance Procedure works. Since we focus on the thymus area, our understanding of the function of this gland and its corresponding chakra and meridian point is necessary. But first let's have a look at the fundamental belief or practice of allopathic or Western medical practices.

Allopaths, or traditional Western doctors, use sophisticated methods of diagnosis and treatment relying on technology and synthetic drugs. It has many advantages in the treatment of pathogen-born diseases, such as typhoid and cholera, and in the management of 20th century diseases, such as heart disease and cancer. Modern medicine, however, takes a reductionist approach. In other words, it understands the human body and illness by breaking it down into separate parts or symptoms rather than examining the whole. When we treat the body as a whole, which is what I do, it is referred to as "holistic treatment" or "holistic medicine."

Allopathic means "treating sickness oppositely." When applied to medical practices, allopathic means giving a drug for a symptom that causes an opposite reaction in the body. For example, treating diarrhoea with a drug to slow the bowels is a common allopathic practice to relieve the symptom of diarrhoea without regard to the condition causing this imbalance in the first place.

This is, of course, the predominant form of medicine practiced in modern societies, and it is responsible, as I said earlier, for the management of 20th century ailments. It has, through its rigorous use of research and experimental practices, helped to extend the life expectancy for many generations and has helped to eradicate or alleviate many diseases with the discovery of treatments like antibiotics. These should be limited to the treatment of bacterial infections, but at times become a "cure all" for any misunderstood ailment. Overuse of antibiotics gives the infection a resistance to them. When they're needed for another bacterial condition, they won't work on the individual who has taken too many antibiotics for the wrong reasons. Also, nature has created new strains of bacteria that are resistant to the drugs prescribed for the less resistant strains, and the cycle continues.

Allopathic medicine does have its place in the world for a variety of diseases and conditions, but it has introduced several negative aspects into health as well. Allopathic medicine breaks down the body into separate parts and often disregards the connection of the various systems to the rest of the body. As a result, it has created a wide acceptance of "side-effects" from treatments. Often the synthetic remedies and prescriptions introduced into the body will cause harm and damage to other organs and systems. In some cases, the treatment may be worse than the disease, with side effects ranging from "liver damage" to suicidal tendencies.

There is a growing trend in Western medicine to view the body holistically as in ancient and Eastern medicine and seek the cause of the "dis-ease" in the body. If the body is imbalanced, it is not at ease, and the whole body should be addressed.

Go Back — The Origin of the Word Thymus (Behavioural Kinesiology)

Dr. John Diamond's book, *Your Body Doesn't Lie*, gives us insight into the ancients' understanding of the thymus. He writes, "In the second century, Galen gave the name thymus to the pinkish-grey two-lobed organ in the chest because, it is said, it reminded him of a bunch of thyme." But the thyme plant itself was so named because it was burned as incense to the gods. Thymus, from the Greek word *thymos*, has deeper origins. Tracing it back beyond the times of Socrates and Plato, the very word *thymos* comes from Indo-European root *dheu*, which is the root word of a wide variety of derivatives meaning to "rise into flames," "to rise into smoke," and "to rise in a cloud of smoke." In Sanskrit, the word was *dhuma*, which gives us the words "fume" and "perfume." The practice of burning incense, a sacrifice to the gods, produced a rising column of smoke.

The word thymus is affiliated with this sacred practice of making a "smoke" offering to the gods, and the connection with this spiritual offering is then tied to the events, physical actions, reactions, and emotions all taking place in the chest. This makes the thymus the "inner altar." It was viewed as the location of aspiration, songs of praise, spirit, and putting out of love from the physical, bodily plane toward the spiritual, metaphysical plane. It was the breath or the very soul on which a man's energy and courage relied. Therefore, the thymus is the seat of life-energy.

Dr. Diamond explains later developments of the understanding of the thymus in Western medicine:

Modern medical science has not always understood the function of the thymus gland.... Now, medicine recognizes the thymus gland is closely related to the immune system, stress, and general well-being.

Earlier this century, it was thought the thymus gland had no function beyond puberty. It was simply a delusion fostered by finding during autopsy that the gland was quite small. It is now known that in response to acute stress such as infection, it can shrivel to half the size within 24 hours. Earlier, doctors thought that after puberty the thymus had no useful function, and in

many young children it was excised! This destroyed a vital part
of their immune systems, allowing them to become susceptible
to infections and chronic disease. Later in the 1950s and after
research, it became clear that children naturally have large thymus
glands and some dying from serious illness or great physical stress
had died before the gland had time to shrink.

After puberty, the thymus diminishes in size because it is
no longer concerned with growth. Any further shrinkage is due
to stress and other factors. The dramatic shrinkage of the thymus
gland in a person undergoing stress is not fully understood.
Within a day of severe injury or sudden illness, millions of
lymphocytes are destroyed and the thymus shrinks to half its
size. This part of the general reaction to stress is described by Dr.
Hans Seyle. We also know that the thymus continues to secrete
hormones and T cells until late in life. This role is known as
immunological surveillance, so another function has been added
to the so-called "inactive" thymus gland.

It is only recently that the immunological functions of this
gland have been understood. It has the role of a master controller
that directs life-giving and healing energies of the body, and is
strongly influenced by an individual's physical environment, social
relationships, food, and posture.

How Then Do We Heal the Overstressed Thymus Gland?

According to Renee Brodie in *Let Light into Your Heart with
Colour and Sound*, "Our immune system functions more effectively
when we are happy and creative and affects every cell in our body
when its energy flow is harmonious." When we feel out-of-sorts, or
unwell, the cells of the immune system do not "ring true," and this

will affect every part of us. We see now how important the thymus is to our well-being.

The thymus is the first organ of the body to be affected by stress. It is also the first organ to be affected at an energy level by an emotional state. The thymus gland may thus be thought of as the link between the mind and body. Besides being affected by stress and emotional states, the thymus is strongly influenced by the individual's physical environment, social relationships, food, and posture. The way you feel will show you which factors in each of these categories lower or raise your life-energy.

From here, we can see how to put this information to use in a simple yet effective way to begin to balance ourselves. Using your feelings list from Chapter Two, examine which areas in your life need more life-energy. A major discovery of behavioural kinesiology is that the thymus gland monitors and regulates energy flow in the energy system. When stress affects the thymus, it cannot do its job properly, and an imbalance must occur. Ultimately, there will be physical damage to a particular part of the body. We know that through the stimulation and attention paid to the thymus/heart chakra, we can work toward balancing this energy centre, and therefore the immune system, until it is 100% perfect. Balance is a state of perfection.

Chakras and Meridians

To understand how emotions can cause energy blocks in the tissues of our body, it is useful to have insight into the Eastern philosophy of the subtle energy fields called chakras and the systems of body circuits called meridians. You may have heard phrases such as, "balancing the chakras," "out of balance," "running the meridians," or "too yin and too yang," but do you know what these words and phrases mean? The following pages

THE BALANCE PROCEDURE

will give you a basic introduction and understanding of chakras and meridians and bring to your attention their complexity and importance, which may in turn inspire you to want to learn more.

"The chakras are specialised energy centres which connect us to the multidimensional universe," says Richard Gerber in his book *Vibrational Medicine*. He goes on to say, "The chakras are dimensional portals within the subtle bodies which take in and process energy of a higher vibrational nature so that it may be properly assimilated and used to transform the body."

Chakras are energy centres and are often depicted as spinning circles at certain points on the human body. Each of the seven chakras corresponds to a physical location, symbol, and colour. Below is a basic diagram of the chakras as understood in Eastern medical practices, yogic practices and meditation. These ideas have carried over into Western medical and traditional practices, too.

THE SEVEN CHAKRAS

Chakra.com, an online source for learning about this ancient wisdom, has defined the chakras and broken each one's functions down very simply.

The word *chakra* is Sanskrit for "wheel or disk" and signifies one of seven basic energy centres in the body. Each of these centres correlates to major nerve ganglia branching forth from the spinal column. In addition, the chakras also correlate to levels of consciousness, archetypal elements, developmental stages of life, colours, sounds, body functions, and much, much more.

Chakra Seven: Violet
Thought, Universal Identity, Oriented to Self-knowledge

This is the crown chakra that relates to consciousness as pure awareness. It is our connection to the greater world beyond, to a timeless, spaceless place of all-knowing. When developed, this chakra brings us knowledge, wisdom, understanding, spiritual connection, and bliss.

Chakra Six: Indigo
Light, Archetypal Identity, Oriented to Self-reflection

This chakra is known as the brow chakra or third eye centre. It is related to the act of seeing, both physically and intuitively. As such, it opens our psychic faculties and our understanding of archetypal levels. When healthy, it allows us to see clearly, in effect letting us "see the big picture."

Chakra Five: Blue
Sound, Creative Identity, Oriented to Self-expression

This is the chakra located in the throat and is thus related to communication and creativity. Here we experience the world symbolically through vibration, such as the vibration of sound representing language.

Chakra Four: Green or Pink
Air, Social Identity, Oriented to Self-acceptance

This chakra is called the heart chakra and is the middle chakra in a system of seven. It is related to love and is the integrator of opposites in the psyche: mind and body, male and female, persona and shadow, ego and unity. A healthy fourth chakra allows us to love deeply, feel compassion, and have a deep sense of peace and centeredness. This chakra is often referred to as the "Rainbow Bridge." This is because it is a "bridge" between the three lower, more physical chakras, and the three higher, more spiritual chakras.

61

Chakra Three: Yellow
Fire, Ego Identity, Oriented to Self-definition

This chakra is known as the power chakra, located in the solar plexus. It rules our personal power, will, and autonomy, as well as our metabolism. When healthy, this chakra brings us energy, effectiveness, spontaneity, and non-dominating power.

Chakra Two: Orange
Water, Emotional Identity, Oriented to Self-gratification

The second chakra, located in the abdomen, lower back, and sexual organs, is related to the element water, and to emotions and sexuality. It connects us to others through feeling, desire, sensation, and movement. Ideally, this chakra brings us fluidity and grace, depth of feeling, sexual fulfillment, and the ability to accept change.

Chakra One: Red
Earth, Physical Identity, Oriented to Self-preservation

Located at the base of the spine, this chakra forms our foundation. It represents the element earth and is therefore related to our survival instincts and to our sense of grounding and connection to our bodies and the physical plane. Ideally, this chakra brings us health, prosperity, security, and dynamic presence.

62

There are several items of note in this basic description of the chakras. Each one is described above with the colour and issues it is associated with and for which it is responsible. Also of note are the physical locations of each chakra. Each corresponds to a physical location on the human body, which affects the nervous system. Traditional science recognises the nervous system as the source through which our brain communicates to each organ and movement, whether voluntary or involuntary, via impulses of energy. Not only is there a physical correspondence to each chakra, but there is also an association with energy centres. A wide variety of sources is available for information on this subject because it is accepted and used by millions of people around the globe.

THE BALANCE PROCEDURE

The chakras, in collaboration with the meridian system, transform and relate higher vibrational energies that are essential for proper growth and the maintenance of health — the main contributor to length and quality of life. The relationship between energy, chakras, and colours can be described in the following way: Energy, on entering the crown chakra, is relayed to the spinal cord and nerve ganglia along the body's central axis. As the energy moves to the lower chakras, the subtle energy currents are distributed to the appropriate organs and body parts. Remember that each chakra is associated with a different vibrational frequency.

Meridians

The concept of meridians is a bit more complex. The website, www.about.com, simplifies this understanding for the layperson.

63

The human body is a natural energy source that generates electrical energy within the ionic environment of cells and tissues. Body fluids contain electrically-charged ions that can cause a current to flow. Body meridians are thought to contain a colourless, free-flowing, non-cellular fluid, which contains this electrical energy throughout the body.

The body's circuit of electrical energy is divided into 12 main meridians, six on each side of the body; they are connected to one of the internal organs and have a greater effect on that organ. Although the meridians are categorised in terms of the organs and tissues they supply, they are thought to form a single continuous circuit which conveys the electromagnetic energy throughout the body.

The meridians are grouped in pairs: one yin and one yang. Yin and yang represent in Chinese medicine a duality of oneness. It is a way of expressing opposite and complimentary states of energy such hot and cold. The term yin is applied to characteristics that are cool, wet, passive, introverted, and female. The term yang is a general term used to describe characteristics that are hot, dry, active, extroverted, and male. The terms used to describe yin and yang are relative rather than absolute states. Meridians are also classified as yin or yang according to the direction in which they flow on the surface of the body. When standing with the arms above the head, all yin meridians flow upwards, from the earth, while yang meridians flow downwards, from the sun.

Each meridian is paired with a yin or yang counterpart as indicated in the table below:

64

YIN	YANG
Lung	Large Intestine
Heart	Small Intestine
Pericardium	Triple Warmer
Spleen	Stomach
Liver	Gall Bladder
Kidney	Bladder

Meridians interconnect deep within the torso and have an internal branch and surface branch. The section worked on is the surface branch, which is accessible to touch techniques.

THE BALANCE PROCEDURE

In addition to the 12 main meridians, there are two additional ones, often referred to as the storage vessels. They are called the Conception Vessel (yin) and Governing Vessel (yang). They run directly up the back and front of the body to the upper and lower lip. They help create balance among the other 12 meridians by dispersing excess chi energy to deficient meridians. They also help unite the meridians by allowing energy to adjust when there is a blockage.

With the Balance Procedure, we work primarily with the Conception Vessel (CV) meridian. Along each meridian are a varying number of pressure points. The Balance Procedure practitioners work with CV 19, CV 18, and CV 17. The English name for CV 19 is Purple Palace, the command tower of the heart over the ascension of the tree of life. The English name for CV 18 is Jade Court, the palace of treasures, blessing of the immortal stone, and expansion into the brilliance of being. Lastly, CV17 is called the Chest Centre, within the inner realms, on the central Dias, the ancient face of wisdom. These points are all located on the centre of the chest, which is a natural point of the body that we touch when you need to balance.

The Balance Procedure is diverse and fascinating if explored with an open mind. All the answers to your imbalances lie within you; you have the power to be happy, healthy, and fulfilled. The Balance Procedure can also show you great wisdom, which can have a positive effect on everyone you meet. The Balance Procedure can help you bring about positive change within you if you are willing to embrace that change. However, if you hold onto negative thoughts and behavioural patterns, they will only give you short-term symptomatic relief at best. It is your birthright to find health and balance, but you must actively claim that birthright for it to become reality.

Colour and Sound:
An Intimate Part of Our Lives

Everything in the universe vibrates colour; light and sounds are manifestations of that vibration. When something vibrates at certain frequency, it emits light. If it vibrates at another frequency, it emits sound. Pure colours and pure sounds are pleasing to the eye and ear. If you could see a disease in terms of colour, it would be a mass of dark or discordant colours. Likewise, if you could hear a disease, it would be perceived as a jumble of inharmonious noise. You can use the harmonious vibrations of colour, light, and sound to restore the balance within you. Colours and sounds offer the body a harmonious pattern to match its own energies. Start to become aware of the colours, sounds, and light around you. Do some colours or sounds make you feel uncomfortable? Do others lift you and make you feel warm? Look around and start to experience colour, sound, and light; this will lead you to perceive the subtle vibrations emanating from you. Guiding vibrations can help you to discover happiness, health, and fulfillment.

In his book, *Healing with Colour and Light*, Theo Gimbel, under whom I had the pleasure and privilege to study, uses "colourful" language to show how imperative it is for us to recognise the impact colour and light have in our lives. He tells us:

Colour influences our very being during each day that we live — the gentle light of a sunrise contrasts with the stark light of a mid-morning, noon, and mid-afternoon to gently tone down in the early evening. Our physical bodies require the differing energy vibrations that we emit at various times of the day.

THE BALANCE PROCEDURE

Using colour for healing was part of the ancient wisdom and was taught and practiced in ancient Egypt, Greece, China, Tibet, and India. It was part of the Mayan culture and the teachings of the North American Indians, as well.

The Greek schools of Pythagoras and Plato were influenced by the ancient teachings, but this all disappeared in the West during the Dark Ages. It was not until the 19th century that the work of Newton and Goethe revived interest in the properties of light and colour.

It is amusing to see that the period labelled "the Dark Ages" was a time when people considered colour irrelevant. With the Age of Enlightenment came renewed interest in the properties of light and colour, and the educated population began to look at colour from a scientific perspective. This interest continued, of course, and Gimbel tells us about how one of the greatest scientific minds of all time "played" with light, and we cannot consider light without also considering colour.

Einstein proved that light is composed of small packets of energy called quanta. These quanta he referred to as photons. Therefore, light energy moves in discrete packages called photons and this movement may be in a wave form.

The colours of the spectrum are composed of photons — the longer the wavelength, the more spaced-out the photons. In the colours blue, indigo, and violet, the wavelengths are short with compacted photons; therefore, these colours possess more energy. The colours at the other end of the light spectrum, red, orange, and yellow, have long wavelengths and therefore less energy.

Einstein made the statement, "All forms of matter are light waves in motion." If you examine this in terms of the quantum theory, it seems so relevant. We as human beings are beings made of light energy and therefore of energy vibrations.

Theo Gimbel's beautiful words regarding the nature of the energy of the universe are difficult to summarise or paraphrase and still maintain the visual imagery he creates with language. His words are as vivid as the colours he sees in nature. He beautifully paints for us a picture of the way colour envelops our world *and our physical form.*

The power of colour is a part of the natural energy of the universe. As part of the spectrum of natural energies emanating from the sun, colour surrounds us. The healing power of sunlight via colour is a vibrational gift of nature. It fills our subtle and physical bodies and interacts with our own energies. Reflect on how good it feels to have the sun on your back. Patterns of energy interactions within and around the human body are similar to those that occur around every living entity in nature.

Colour has subtle energetic healing properties and is of the simplest ingredient found in nature. Colour is a gift of evolution. It influences our thoughts, our social behaviour, our health, and our relationships; in fact, we cannot live without the light which contains all colours. If you put a plant in a cupboard and shut out the light, it withers and dies. Colour can be measured. All organs and parts of our bodies when they are healthy hold to a particular set of harmonious vibrations. It has been proven that it is part and parcel of the psychic and physical make up of human beings. Young children interpret their environment in terms of colour before they interpret it in terms of shape. When pre-schoolers are asked to sort coloured shapes, they automatically divide it according to colour, rather than shape. Boys and girls, however, tend to differ slightly in that girls will maintain the colour response as a criterion for a longer time. Boys will begin to sort the colourful shapes according to shape at an earlier age. Colour associations contribute to the young child's consciousness. As they grow older, feelings, memories, and meanings are attached to experiences of colour, and this results in colour becoming a feature of the subconscious. The association of particular colours with a happy, sad, joyous, angry, or frightening experience builds up colour preferences. In this way, colour has physical, physiological, emotional, and spiritual connotations.

Our responses to colour are governed by deep-seated associations that have been either conditioned by our experiences or inherited from the past. Certain phraseology has a cultural bias; for example, consider the phrases, "green with envy," "seeing red," or "feeling blue." This tends to indicate an intuitive connection between feelings and colour used to describe the feeling. What is surprising is that responses to colour are surprisingly similar the world over.

The ways in which we respond to colour — through the heart (intuition, emotion), the mind (brain, intellect), the body and its senses follow the path of all our experiences, which are met first by the emotional response generated by the heart — the seat of the intuition. Once we have made an emotional, intuitive response to a situation or encounter, our intellect is activated by the brain. Our immediate response is analysed by the intellect, which controls the subsequent response of the whole body. We respond to colour with each of our senses, each sense transmitting information about the outside world to the brain. The brain then processes the information for meaning and relays it to the conscious feeling aspect.

69

Our clothes are colourful and we eat colourful food. It is seldom that we experience a colourless existence. If we do, we evidence symptoms of deprivation. Inmates in a prison environment who are confined to dark solitary cells usually emerge from these with certain psychological disturbances. As human beings, we need both light and darkness, just as seeds need both darkness to germinate and light to grow.

Colour dominates our senses. It affects us all; we reflect our environment and well-being in terms of colour. We tend to use colour to describe our physical health, moods, and attitudes; for example, we often refer to "feeling blue," "being green with envy," "having a golden opportunity," "being red or purple with rage." Do bear in mind that each sense can enhance a colour experience, and colour enhances the experience of the senses. For example, when you close your eyes and hear a piece of music with the sounds of the waves, what colours are brought to mind? Another example: with your eyes closed you hear the sounds of a steam locomotive; what colours do you see? Sight enhances colour awareness the most because it takes place at a physical level. If you, however, close your eyes, it helps to increase your awareness of colour images. The sense of smell and colour are closely linked: how often have you not smelled something rancid and said that the smell turns you green? The link between colour and sound was familiar to the Druids who, at the winter solstice, retreated to their caves for three days. On the third day, each cave was flooded with light and sound that seemed to have no source. By chanting, the Druids produced the full spectrum of harmonic overtones, which created a state of awareness that "let in" the full spectrum of light.

In summary, we can see that colour has been recognised at various points in history for its profound effect on human beings, from our moods to our thoughts and memories and, as Theo Gimbel has pointed out, to all of our senses, not just our sight. Because colour has the impact on us that it does, we can and should use it to best suit our health and to help create harmony, or balance, in our lives.

How You Can Work With Colour

When you look at the mechanism that validates the effects of colour, review the following:

- There are different vibrational frequencies of colour. Reds vibrate at the longest wavelengths, have the lowest frequencies, and the least energy. Violets have the shortest wavelengths, highest frequencies, and the most energy.

- As humans, we are multidimensional beings, having higher dimensional light bodies, which are vibrating at different frequencies and relate to colour vibrations. In other words, the different subtle bodies, or auric fields, have different luminous colours.

71

- The subtle body and physical body are connected by the chakras. Chakras also vibrate at different frequencies, which once again can be related to colour.

- Once the colour vibration has been transformed into accessible energy by the chakras, this life-force energy is relayed through the meridian system in the body via the various organs.

Two Colour Breathing Exercises

This is a useful balancing exercise. Make yourself comfortable, relax your body, and quiet your mind.

- **Breathe at a rate that is comfortable for you. Establish a natural rhythm and focus on your breathing until you have cleared your mind.**

- **Hold a positive image of yourself. Bring a colour to mind — your intuition will select the appropriate colour if you are calm and focused.**

- **When the colour comes to mind, breathe in that colour. Visualise that colour entering the thymus/ heart chakra and spreading throughout your body. As you breathe out, visualise the colour.**

- **Repeat this three times. Single colour breathing refers to specific needs.**

Red	Breathe in red for vitality. It brings energy and increases sexuality, strength, and will-power. Breathe out turquoise.
Orange	Breathe in orange for joy, happiness, and fun. Breathe out blue.
Yellow	Breathe in yellow to increase your objectivity and intellectual powers. Breathe out violet.
Green	Breathe in green to cleanse and feel balanced. Breathe out magenta.

THE BALANCE PROCEDURE

Turquoise	Breathe in turquoise to counteract inflammations and fever and to strengthen the immune system. Breathe out red.
Blue	Breathe in blue for relaxation and peace and in cases of insomnia. Breathe out orange.
Violet	Breathe in violet to increase self-respect and feelings of dignity and beauty. Breathe out yellow.
Magenta	Breathe in magenta to let go of any obsessive images, thoughts, and memories. Breathe out green.

Life is all about living in harmony and being in balance with all that surrounds us.

If there is light in the soul,
there will be beauty in the person.
If there is beauty in the person,
there will be harmony in the house.
If there is harmony in the house,
there will be order in the nation.
If there is order in the nation,
there will be peace in the world.

– Chinese Proverb

CHAPTER FOUR

Keeping the Balance

*There is nothing either good or bad,
but thinking makes it so.*

– William Shakespeare

Every thought you have, positive or negative, sends energy out to the universe. Those vibrations attract other vibrations to themselves that return back to the source, which means that "as you sow, so shall you reap." If you think negative thoughts, you will attract negativity to you. If you think positive, pleasing thoughts, your life will become more beautiful and harmonious. Your very thoughts are influencing the pattern of your life. Take full responsibility for your every thought, word and action because they each transmit real vibrations. Once you do this, you will begin to understand the power that is latent within you. You have the ability to influence the vibrations you send out and those you attract. Once you understand this concept, you will be able to concentrate on learning all you need to make life happy, healthy, and fulfilled rather than fighting the energies created by your own powers of thought.

76

It is possible to attain and remain in a state of health and ease by maintaining harmony at all levels of being: physical, emotional, mental, and spiritual. However, human life presents people with a wide range of experiences that throw the systems out of balance. For the average person, this state of constant balance is not possible, so disease results. We must understand what can cause imbalance in the mind, body, and spirit.

Stress will affect different parts of the body in different people according to where they are most vulnerable, e.g. stomach, neck, head, heart, or back.

Emotions, such as anger, fear, hate, grief, guilt, frustration, and resentment, are harmful if not dealt with. When these are stored rather than expressed, the body reacts and may eventually demonstrate these emotions in the form of physical disease.

Self-created disease is a condition where the "payoff" is greater than the discomfort. For example, poor health can be a means of gaining attention where no other strategy will work. This usually is on a subconscious level. Judgment of personal looks, success, abilities, or behaviour is a cause of distress and consequently of disease.

Dwelling on negativity and negative thoughts can create disease. Energy follows thought, and therefore it is possible to create a disease by "thinking the body into it." Conversely, positive thoughts can assist in "thinking the body into health."

The **life plan** for each person is set, and conscious or unconscious conflict with the plan will lead to stress and ill-health. The plan may include working out karma, and the physical condition is part of that process.

THE CYCLE OF STRESS AND DISTRESS

THREAT (real or imagined danger)

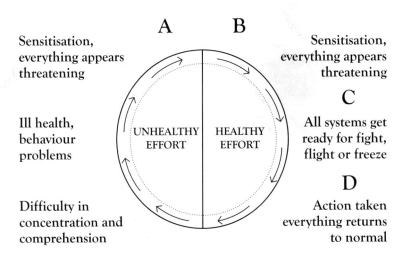

A   B

Sensitisation, everything appears threatening

Sensitisation, everything appears threatening

C

Ill health, behaviour problems

UNHEALTHY EFFORT   HEALTHY EFFORT

All systems get ready for fight, flight or freeze

D

Difficulty in concentration and comprehension

Action taken everything returns to normal

The Cycle Can Be Broken At Several Points

a. Change or avoid the situation.

b. Change mental attitude using the Balance Procedure

c. Change bodily reaction using the Balance Procedure as a relaxation response.

d. Use up stress chemicals. Take exercise.

Stress

One of the biggest complaints people have these days is that they are stressed. Our lives seem to be relentlessly demanding and hectic. Individuals can find that the impact of stress blights their health and happiness. However, stress is a complex phenomenon; it can't be painted in black and white. Neither lack of stress nor excessive stress is good for you. We have been conditioned to see stress as purely negative because of catchphrases like "stress kills." It is my belief that all the discussion of stress and its associated symptoms can add to the stresses of life. It is possible to manage stress without becoming slaves to therapy, drugs, or other medical or scientific remedies. By no means is this book intended to be a substitute for legitimate medical or psychological diagnosis; however, common sense will be the guiding principle of the day. Common sense will form the foundation of the coping strategies that will emerge from the reading.

It is perfectly natural for everyone to experience the stressors of modern life. Stressors do exist and will continue to exist. We cannot eliminate them, but we can learn to become balanced and calm. Being in this state whenever we need to be will lessen the impact these stressors can have on us. Remember, it is not the event or person that is causing this response, but our reaction to the event or person.

What is Stress?

Stress is the impact, either external or internal, of a demand on a human being. The demand can be positive or negative, and, debatably at the moment, there is no life without stress.

On a physical level, when the brain senses a demand for exertion, it signals the release of various hormones to the endocrine glands around the body. When someone is subjected to stress, input from the five senses travels through the nervous system and triggers the hypothalamus in the brain to send out signals. These signals reach the pituitary gland, which sends a hormonal response to the adrenal gland to release adrenaline into the bloodstream, preparing the body for "fight or flight."

79

The normal functioning of the body is disrupted since a body in a state of stress needs to conserve its energy to propel muscles. The adrenaline coursing through the bloodstream causes blood pressure to rise and muscles to tense. Breathing becomes shallow and rapid, sexual desire and hunger are suppressed, and digestion stops. The brain becomes hyper-alert.

As a temporary expedient, the stress response is vital; but if the situation is prolonged with no release of tension, it can be disastrous. As well as increasing heart rate and blood pressure, the body diverts vital resources from the immune system, and cholesterol levels rise.

The common symptoms of prolonged stress include fatigue, headaches, heartburn, indigestion, hair loss, insomnia, and depression. Some more serious conditions and diseases associated with prolonged stress are acidosis, backache, irritable bowel syndrome, Crohn's disease, kidney failure, and even heart attacks.

Accepting that there are physical and emotional stresses, we can now concentrate on the stresses that relate to you and the way you approach life.

Time

Ask almost anyone what his biggest anxiety is, and he will say "time." As the world gets busier and demands from work and family arise, people believe that one thing we don't have control over is time. We have been programmed into becoming time-conscious. I remember always being told, "Get a move on," "You are such a slowcoach," "It's time for dinner," "Hurry up, Jenny, you'll miss the bus," or "You're always late." Punctuality rates with honesty as a mark of character strength. We go through life believing there is more and more we have to achieve in our working days and our lives. Is this your belief?

Another aspect of time relates to things that are not happening, have never happened, and probably never will happen. Anxiety and worry are future-based, and most are imaginary. One reason we keep worrying is that worry itself creates the illusion that we are doing something about a problem, that we are "working on it." The truth is, worrying is a waste of time. It is not a problem-solving activity. It does not help us set goals for change. It does not give us a plan of action. Worrying doesn't do anything that actually makes a positive difference to our lives. What does worrying do? It makes us feel afraid; it builds up a bad attitude, leads to more worry, and cheats us out of experiencing the NOW in a positive way.

THE BALANCE PROCEDURE

A friend of mine is a writer who works from home on her computer. Recently, while moving her home office, she decided to clean dust out of the computer, as she does frequently in order to keep her machine in tip-top shape. After hooking up her computer, it would not boot up. She was in the middle of two large writing projects she'd not backed up with an outside disk or other medium, and she began to experience stress. Not only would she be delayed in working for several days, but the thought that her computer had crashed and that she had no way to retrieve the projects in progress began to take its toll on her. She tried several times to reopen the tower of her PC to see if she'd knocked anything loose, but, not being a computer expert, she felt an impending sense of doom. Days lost working, beginning from scratch on projects well underway, and an expensive repair job raised her heart rate and brought her tears of fear. She began to submit to the stress. She decided to use the Balance Procedure to regain her composure because she knew nothing would be accomplished by simply breaking down. She repeated the process, and by the third repeat, she literally stood over the tower asking for balance to figure out what was wrong and, if necessary, how to proceed without her computer. Buying a new one was not an option at that moment.

She said she calmed down and "knew everything would be okay." After taking only a few breaths in her state of calm, her phone rang, and a friend was looking for her to join him on an outing. She told him what happened, and he said, "Look again to see if you knocked something loose." Though she was quite sure she'd checked her connections, she obliged and found that the memory card had become ever so slightly dislodged. She clicked it in again and reconnected the computer. She reported tears of joy when she "heard the glorious Windows music."

All information was still intact. Nothing was lost.

The point here is that sometimes we are incapacitated by stress and not able to take the appropriate action to remedy our situations. When we are in a state of balance, then the appropriate information can flow. It is just like in my friend's computer. When it could finally locate its "memory," it could then function properly. The computer was in balance. Stress literally blocks the flow of information for balance, and restoring that balance can open up the flow of energy in the body and its environs.

Another source of stress is "time that has passed." Sadness about events that happened long ago, regrets about things said or done, disappointments over relationships that may go back to your childhood, anger that has never been resolved, and limiting beliefs that we learned as we were growing up can captivate the imagination and send it on long journeys of useless toil. It is interesting to note, however, that the aspect of past time at *this* very moment does not exist.

There is one moment in time when you can have no worries or anxieties about the future nor regrets about the past – and that moment is NOW. "now" has no beginning or end and exerts no pressure. By living in the "Now," your stressful thoughts about the past and the future will stop.

In our nonstop, frenetic lives, many of us let stress levels build and build until we're forced to take a break. It seems that we need to learn to relax daily. What counts is not leisure time and taking holidays, but how we spend our daily lives.

How do you spend your workdays? You may grit your teeth every day and think, "Just two more weeks until my holiday. I will be able to unwind and get rid of all this stress." The bad news is that reaching boiling point on a daily basis is bad for you. Letting it build up until it boils over forces you to stop everything for several days. This doesn't work, and it may even be dangerous.

THE BALANCE PROCEDURE

Chronic accumulation of stress and anxiety is bad for your mind, body, and spirit. As already stated, the effects on the physical body also undermine the immune system, leaving us more vulnerable to colds and to even more serious diseases; it also makes us put on weight and gives premature wrinkles.

Do you know anyone that is bombarded by urgent requests from all sides but never stops smiling, as if they can plunge into stressful situations for a few minutes when required and then emerge unscathed? What does this mean when some people are unaffected by stress?

When someone is unaffected by stress, they are centred; or better, their energies are centred, and they are invulnerable to stress. To remain centred at all times is one of our primary goals. If you want to manage your stress levels, don't wait until the holidays. Deal with it daily. Once you grasp this realisation and learn the Balance Procedure, you'll gain a tremendous sense of control over your reactions, your health, and your life. Stress may be unavoidable in this life, but that does not mean that distress is inevitable. It isn't.

The Balance Procedure gives the body awareness. It reconnects our mind and body so that we can function as an efficient, balanced, and productive unit. The body gets its energy from the food and nutrients we consume. Nowadays, most body energy is wasted on stress and anxiety, strain and boredom; there is less energy for actual life and learning. Using this process daily is the key to reducing the amount of stress in our lives. This is the key to calm us down, so we get to sleep properly again, eat properly again, feel strong and healthy, and easily handle surprises and the daily shocks of living as we flow swiftly from one experience to the other.

5

The History of Meridian Techniques and the Evolution of the Balance Procedure

Today, we have a wide variety of modern energy meridian techniques that apply the ancient knowledge of meridian channels and points, first recorded in 5000 B.C., and often incorporate more recent ideas and trends. Many of these are hybrids of the old and the new. This ancient knowledge has been developed in modern times by several practitioners with a range of skills and experiences, leading to the development of modern energy meridian therapies.

In the 1960s and 1970s, the links among muscle strength, meridians, organ and gland health, and psychology were explored and led to the development of muscle testing as a diagnostic tool and to the field of kinesiology. Muscle testing studies the body's strength and weakness when given certain stimulation, such as herbal remedies, essential oils, and colour, light, or sound applications. It simply tests the effect on the physical energy of the body when subjected to certain things. At a basic level, muscle testing uses the theory that when a muscle is strong, it is the truth. If it is weak, then it is not truth. There are other tests you can use, and though muscle testing is not a basic part of the Balance Procedure, it can be very useful in assessing progress and deciding how to move forward.

Here are a few different ways muscle testing can be explained. Often a person stands upright with their feet shoulder-width apart. Many different muscles could be used for the test. The easiest is usually to use the big deltoid muscles of the arms. The client stretches one arm straight out in front of them or straight out to the side. The facilitator instructs the client to repeat a statement (for example, "My name is Jane") and to resist while they press down on the arm. If the arm holds strong while being pressed down, it is a true statement, or if it gives in and becomes weak, it is not true. There is a certain ability to sensing it, but once a person has got it, it is a very definite sign. The interesting thing is that muscle testing works just as well on mental or emotional issues as on physical body parts. You can put your attention on something and then test for a weak or strong response. That is something we can use. Keep in mind that statements are taken literally, so they have to be worded precisely. The body will give answers to things that are submerged and unknown to the conscious processes, and it will give answers without being biased by wishful thinking or social manoeuvring.

Self-testing can be done in various ways. One way is to touch the thumb to the middle finger of each hand to form two rings, linked through each other. First say something true, "My name is [give your name]." At the same time, pull the linked fingers of the right hand against those of the left, but don't allow them to separate. Then say something false, "My name is [give someone else's name]." Repeat the same gesture as before with the fingers, but this time deliberately separate them, as though they were flying apart or repelling each other. You don't need to make the true and false statements aloud. Doing this silently is okay, as long as you do it each time.

Another way to self-test is the sticky/smooth test. I mostly use this with my clients, as most are able to do it easily with a little practice. Rub one of your finger pads across your thumb pad, using simple yes/no statements. Your action will be either sticky for "no" or smooth for "yes." It is a simple test that can be used anywhere. The idea is to train the mind in different responses for truth and falsehood. If you practice this for 10 or 15 minutes a day, you should be able to develop the response within a few weeks.

Muscle testing will not provide accurate responses to certain statements — about the future, for example. You'll get a response, but the response to, "This answer is reliable" will be "no." It is quite fun to play with muscle testing to see how this simple practice works. Once the learner is comfortable with this sort of testing, there are untold numbers of ways to use this to find balancing remedies and solutions for anything confronting the individual. Muscle testing can be helpful for testing your responses to beliefs or blocks on relationships and occupations, among other subjects. The muscles really do react to what one thinks and feels and imagines. For further information on muscle testing, Dr. John Diamond's book, *Your Body Doesn't Lie,* is an excellent source. When working by yourself, you can also use a pendulum to give a positive or negative response.

In 1981, Dr. Roger Callahan, a cognitive psychologist who studied kinesiology under John Diamond, was also investigating Eastern health practices based on the theory in Chinese medicine that energy flows along meridian lines in the body.

In an attempt to help Mary, his patient with a water phobia, he tested his theory. He asked her to think about water and tap with two fingers on the point that connected with the stomach meridian. Much to his surprise, her fear of water completely disappeared. For the next 10 years, Callahan continued to expand and evolve his discovery, which he named "Thought Field Therapy" (TFT). He developed a number of brief treatments or "algorithms." Algorithms are step-by-step procedures, or sequences of body taps, geared to particular conditions that patients can perform on themselves to get rid of negative emotional responses

In 1991, Gary Craig and Dr. Larry Nims both trained with Roger Callahan. In 1995, Gary Craig, an engineer and lay preacher, developed the Emotional Freedom Technique (EFT). He simplified the use of the 15 meridian points that Callahan had identified for all emotional responses and developed a technique that all people could learn easily. Since then, other therapies have been developed that apply meridian and energy principles. Larry Nims developed Be Set Free Fast (BSFF), Tapas Fleming developed Tapas Acupressure Treatment (TAT), and EmoTrance emerged from the work of Silvia Hartmann. There are now many other "cousins" leading to the formation of the Association for Meridian Energy Therapies (AAMET) in the United Kingdom by Tam and Mary Llewellyn (www.aamet.org).

Meridian Energy Therapies have provided practitioners the world over with a new collection of groundbreaking techniques for providing quick and permanent relief from negative emotional states.

I was introduced to Emotional Freedom Technique by Jacquie Crooks. Within the first hour of the workshop she led, I knew my life had changed forever. In the workshop, we were asked to choose a small problem to work with. My particular problem was food-related. I still couldn't stop my poor eating habits, even after years of being a Weight Watchers leader and following every diet. Even though I really wanted to, I couldn't stop overeating or binging, and I couldn't commit to the food that would give me life-energy. I felt dread and anxiety from just the memory of making my packed lunch that morning and the thought of eating it in front of others in the class, who were mostly other therapists I knew and admired. Jacquie and I worked together with this, and I had "a three-minute wonder," as it is sometimes known in the EFT world. I was able get to the core issue and release the guilt that I had been holding onto since childhood. I am truly grateful that I experienced freedom from the guilt and shame that had run my life. EFT changed my life forever. I had never heard of EFT before that day, but I knew from that moment what a powerful and profound technique it was, and it worked! It gave me freedom. My life has not been the same since.

As a therapist and a teacher, I decided to spread the word about EFT. This then took me to learning other Meridian Energy Therapies. I had the great pleasure of studying Tapas Acupressure Technique (TAT) with the developer Tapas Fleming, and I become a practitioner and trainer. I also studied Be Set Free Fast, which was developed by Larry Nims.

I am still taken aback by how successful Meridian Energy Therapies are and how they work on attitude, choices and memories. Since learning Meridian Energy Therapies, I have been passionate about spreading the word. As a teacher, I have been able to train students at a level they never thought possible. As a therapist, I have seen people transform their lives – little short of miracles. I have had more "thank you" letters doing energy therapy work than I have had doing any other work in the past 20 years.

Energy or meridian techniques are causing a revolution in complimentary medicine as we know it. People are realising the benefits of these techniques, which are far less invasive than allopathic practices. These are exciting times as new techniques are constantly evolving and developing that work even quicker! It is my intention that "The Balancing Procedure Course" will introduce you to a new technique, which is both simpler and more intricate than other techniques and is an essential part of everybody's "toolbox." Learn the Balance Procedure to lift your own experience, to add new sparkle to your life as you communicate with yourself and others, and to be and feel successful in everything you do.

The Balance Procedure

The Balance Procedure is the evolution of my own work with energy or meridian therapies. As a practitioner of a variety of therapies for a number of years, it is only natural that my own findings and experiences would lead me to adjusting the ideas and techniques I studied into what I find works best.

THE BALANCE PROCEDURE

In the Balance Procedure, we start with the heart chakra, which corresponds with the thymus gland on the physical level. This point is used in the Balance Procedure. In traditional Tibetan teaching, the thymus and heart chakra share the same energy. The heart/thymus chakra links our physical and non-physical aspects. This chakra is the centre of love, harmony, and balance. A very crucial point to understand about the thymus gland is that it is the physical centre of immunity in the body. Scientists have studied areas of the brain that may influence the performance of the immune system. Already much has been learned, since we know that nerves pass from the brain stem directly into the thymus gland in the neck. That is a short route, relatively speaking. The thymus gland is the "Throne of Immunity." These nerve fibres indicate that messages can pass from the brain to the thymus and vice versa. What sort of signals are dispatched along these newly discovered fibres is unknown, but they are not there by chance. Something important is going on.

Like all organs, limbs, and systems in the body, messages pass from the thymus to the brain and visa versa. It is for this very reason that we must communicate good, life-affirming things to our thymus and heart, because they can't keep a secret! They *are going* to tell the brain, and the brain tells everything else in the body. When these messages start circulating in the body, the various systems may react if they buy into it.

If we beat ourselves up with negativity and guilt, what then do you think occurs with the immune system? Be kind to yourself. Love yourself. Tell yourself you are perfect and that you are whole. There is nothing broken in you. You can centre yourself easily; allow the chi to flow, restoring your perfection. I'll go into the Balance Procedure in a step-by-step fashion in the next chapter, but you can begin to use the fundamentals of it right now. Start asking, "What do I want," instead of "What don't I want?"

Once you learn the Balance Procedure, you'll be able to feel that state of peace, calm, and overall well-being. It is a good idea to practice finding this place frequently so you can easily identify it when you need to reach it quickly. Then begin to dream. Use your imagination to see yourself in all sorts of scenarios. See yourself hugely successful. See yourself at your ideal size or weight. See yourself free of any bad habit you'd like to let go of, such as smoking, nail-biting, or complaining. The reason I encourage this practice of using the imagination is that thoughts ARE energy, as I've already discussed in the preceding chapter on energy. Thoughts from our brain travel throughout our bodies, and in the words of Mike Dooley on the hit DVD, *The Secret*, "Thoughts become things." Creation of these things and experiences begins with the communication we have with ourselves at the heart level. What we say to the heart/thymus chakras are those things we accept as we want them to be. Choose good thoughts to tell yourself. Your consistent thoughts persist and become your *reality*, so talk to yourself in a way that supports who you want to be. If you find it a lie to tell yourself that you have a lot of money, understand that it is because you've rehearsed the "I'm broke" conversation with yourself for years. Now, change the message and see the fulfillment of your dreams and ambitions in the future!

92

Identify Your Wants

Follow these exercises below to find out your purpose in life. Once you start using your mind and imagination, you'll have a clearer and more focused idea of what you want to be, what you want to do, and what you want to have. Take action now.

What is it you want? Who you want to *be*? What you want to *do*? What do you want to *have*?

What Do You Want?

Use the worksheet at the end of this chapter to write down all of the things that you want. (Use additional sheets of paper if you need to. These can be updated as you grow and learn.) Use your imagination without limitation. You can think of anything at all; go for your dreams. Aim high. Do not complete the column labelled, "What is stopping you?"

Don't worry about whether you "should." "Shoulds" are mostly conditions placed on us from the outside, perceived as real.

Write what you want.

Our imaginations are powerful. We are all image-makers, and we always have been. This is the exciting part of the Balance Procedure. When understood, it can improve every aspect of your life. I have watched people grow as the new ideas register in their consciousness. How are you using your image-making? What results do you have? Everything in your life has come as a direct result of image-making. This is a great mental tool, but most people have learned to use it in a negative way. Imagination is more important than knowledge. Albert Einstein commented on this in an article entitled "What Life Means to Einstein," which appeared in *The Saturday Evening Post* in 1929. "For knowledge is limited, whereas imagination embraces the entire world, stimulating progress, giving birth to evolution." Wallace D. Wattles, the author of *The Science of Getting Rich*, wrote, "This thinking stuff permeates, penetrates and fills the interstices of the cosmos. We can tap into this thinking stuff with our minds and form any image we choose."

The knowledge of image-making eliminates competition from your life by moving you from the competitive plane to the

93

creative plane. "Images" are mental pictures made from thoughts. Are you successful? Are you free from insecurity, both financially and emotionally? Your right to life means your right to have free and unrestricted use of all the things which may be necessary in pursuit of your highest, fullest mental, physical and spiritual well-being.

Our beliefs, both conscious and unconscious, determine our experiences. We can recognize what we believe by noticing the experiences in which we find ourselves.

Are you growing or are you focusing backward? Most people get a short way into their imagination and then stop. If we look at the reason for this, we can soon discover why. When people allow their thoughts to take them into larger fields of action, their conditioning and beliefs evolve in their thought. Possibilities change. When anyone stops enlarging their thoughts, they stop growing. Nothing in the universe ever stops. Watch your thoughts for inactivity. Never see the limitation. Never dwell on the limitation. And above all things, never talk limitation to anyone. The man with the big thoughts is always the man who does big things in life.

Often, when we try to quantify our thoughts, we find them slipping away from us, leaving only a foggy impression of a great idea. The following sections are here to help you to get through the fog.

The Goals

What are you trying to achieve? Do you have a clear idea of what you expect in your life? If you don't have a strong sense of what your purpose is, you will be confused and weak. If you can't see the target, how can you take aim? Understanding exactly what you want from your life is your foundation — a visual map that will give you an outline of your purpose day-by-day. It may change quite radically as your ideas evolve and develop, but this is a start. Your goals are the blueprint from which you construct the life you desire.

Who Do You Want To Be?

Write down the names of at least seven people you like or admire. It can be anyone, a friend, family member, co-worker, celebrity, politician, author, scientist, musician, philosopher, teacher — anyone at all. You can write down real or fictional characters, contemporary or historical. List everyone you like or admire for some reason; it doesn't matter why for now.

Now, write the characteristics or qualities you like or admire about that person next to each name. After you've done this for each person, go through the list of qualities and compile them into a condensed list. Put the qualities that repeat at the top of your list. It could be their honesty, authenticity, compassion, wisdom, laughter, creativity, movement, beauty, inspiration, wisdom, or confidence that you admire. What qualities are you left with? Do you have these qualities? Do you wish you had them? Which do you want to develop more? Are there any qualities on your list that you don't think you possess? Simply being aware of the qualities you want to possess and using your imagination can bring them out in you.

What Do You Want To Do?

Throw all caution to the wind when developing your ideas about your future! What do you want to do? Identify what you want to do using your imagination. You don't have to take anyone else or any other circumstance into consideration for this exercise. Of course, in life, we do need to consider others and our circumstances, but this is a brainstorming exercise. You don't have to worry about time, space, or money, and you have total freedom to be self-indulgent here. This isn't about finding a career, although it may eventually become one. It's about identifying what you enjoy doing. Write down every activity you enjoy doing or would like to experience.

Great thinkers have always known about the importance of imagination:

"They who dream by day are cognizant of many things which escape those who dream only by night."

– Edgar Allan Poe

"You see things and you say 'Why?' But I dream things that never were and I say, why not?"

– George Bernard Shaw

"I believe that imagination is stronger than knowledge — that myth is more potent than history. I believe that dreams are more powerful than facts."

– Robert Fulghum

THE BALANCE PROCEDURE

*"You can't depend on your judgment when
your imagination is out of focus."*

– Mark Twain

Changing your life doesn't need to be "hard work" because the journey is so joyful. As we create more joy and happiness in our lives, we grow more confident. Being more confident, we can reach the deeper structure of our experience, the underlying patterns and beliefs that have driven our behaviour until now. Using the Balance Procedure enables us to "step over the line," to do what we need to do in the world, to create something of benefit to the others we can reach, something to provide us with a worthy epitaph.

I offer workshops to teach the Balance Procedure from scratch. Please visit my website **www.attractingbalance.com** for information on attending or sponsoring an event. It is a life-changing course. Even if you are completely new to "energy techniques," you will finish the day able and excited to use the procedure for yourself, your friends, and your family. You'll get much of it from this book, but we know that all things are in motion and that most of the energy techniques in use today are improved versions of the ancient philosophy. It stands to reason that as I continue this work and get feedback from clients and practitioners, I will add to this exciting, life-enhancing procedure.

The Balance Procedure will help you to:

- **Change your mind to create a positive emotional attitude, which allows positive physical, mental, and spiritual health.**

- Feel real energy for life. Feel energetic, inspired, optimistic, intrigued, trustful, stimulated, eager, hopeful, and joyous.

- Feel better about yourself and your life by eliminating negative beliefs and blocks.

- Pursue your desires by reducing physical and mental stress.

- Make more permanent changes, deal more effectively with change, and take command of your future.

The introductory training is intended to be complete in its own right so that even if you decide to go no further with formal training, you will have gained a precious tool for life, just as I intend with this book. However, we hope you may be inspired to take your learning further and join us in learning new levels of expertise. The basics of the Balance Procedure are simple to learn and are available to everyone.

Awareness is the first step in the Balance Procedure. As you grow in self-awareness, you will better understand why you feel what you feel and why you behave as you behave. That understanding then gives you the opportunity and *freedom* to change those things you'd like to change about yourself and to create the life you want. Without knowing who you are, self-acceptance and change become impossible.

So let's learn the Balance Procedure!

WORKSHEET

What Do I Want?

1. _____
2. _____
3. _____
4. _____
5. _____
6. _____
7. _____

99

Who Do I Want to Be?

Seven People I Admire	Qualities I Admire in Them
1. _____	_____
2. _____	_____
3. _____	_____
4. _____	_____
5. _____	_____
6. _____	_____
7. _____	_____

Top Qualities in Those Admire   Those I Possess   Those I Want to Possess

1. _____   _____   _____

2. _____   _____   _____

3. _____   _____   _____

4. _____   _____   _____

5. _____   _____   _____

6. _____   _____   _____

7. _____   _____   _____

CHAPTER SIX

Principles and Practice of the Balance Procedure

JENNY COX

We all feel challenges in life. They can spur some of us into action, yet for many the idea of a challenge can keep them stuck in certain situations. We may feel powerless to move forward or take control of our lives. The situations and conditions that we think limit our forward motion or growth might feel insurmountable, yet there is liberation in finding a place to begin. It is with a single step that we begin any journey, and the journey toward restoring our lives to balance is no different. It can lead you to balancing your emotions, which will enable you to choose healthy and useful behaviours and interactions. The Balance Procedure presents an inborn, instinctive, effortless way of looking at life and the means to change it if you wish.

The main aim of the Balance Procedure is to be a self-help tool, bringing our lives back into harmony and focus. We all panic or tune out at times. The point is that you get to make a choice. If you opt for being tuned in and focused, you can get there with the Balance Procedure. Everybody can reap the full benefits and learn how to use this simple, effective procedure for transforming the energies that have been blocking their full potential to create and evolve.

102

The Balance Procedure starts with identifying what you want. Do you know what you want? Have you been living your life doing what you think you should want to do, or what you think *other people want you to do*? Do you have regrets that you haven't lived your dreams? Find out what you want NOW. Every day ask yourself the question, "What do I want?" Write down whatever it is. Do you want a better relationship with your spouse, children, or parent? Do you wish to have space for yourself, financial security, world peace, more fun, and more laughter?

I asked for more laughter with my husband many years ago, before I was aware that I was creating my own reality. By the next weekend, we were in London training with Dr. Kataria, a great man from India who is a pioneer and founder of the Laughter Clubs movement all over the world. He developed a technique of laughter therapy based on yoga (www.laughteryoga.org). After the training, we invited him to Cambridge, where the local television network filmed him in a workshop. For a long time after that, Alan and I ran weekly laughter workshops in and around Cambridge. I got what I wanted — laughter with my husband and lots of other people! It was brilliant! Laughter has no language and knows no boundaries. It is incredibly powerful and has great potential for uniting the world. Find out what you want now. After identifying what you want, there are seven simple steps to follow.

The first step in The Balance Procedure is to identify what is blocking you from having what you want. What kind of a feeling is it? Is it tension, cramping, or simply just discomfort or unease? Is it a feeling of frustration or lack of direction? Is it disassociation? Look inside yourself for the negative feeling that is blocking your desire. How much do you believe in it? How painful is it? Where are you feeling it in your body? How do you know that it is true? What do you want to do with it? Do you wish to let it go?

103

A common question I get is, "How do I know I am blocked?" This can be quite a challenge because many of us become so accustomed to the things that hang us up in life that we can't easily identify those things that do prevent us from living the life we want of health, wealth, and overall happiness.

What is blocking you? Only you can figure this out. The exercises in the last chapter were the actions to take to help identify what you want or what you want to do. Return to those lists and see what obstacles are stopping you.

Is it a belief that is blocking you? Beliefs are often so ingrained in us that it may take much effort to remove these blockages, but once you identify them as thought patterns that are not "true" for you, they then become easier and easier to let go of. For example, if you have truly believed all your life that you cannot have good health because you have a family history of various ailments, a belief in sickness is holding you up. You may truly believe that you are doomed to repeat the same maladies that your parents and grandparents suffered from. Even traditional psychology and psychiatry recognize the phenomenon of "anniversary death," a condition in which, for example, a child dies at the same age as his or her parent and from a related cause. You can escape the cycle of sickness in a family unit by changing your belief and taking the steps to remove these blockages.

The second step is measuring the level of discomfort or physical disturbance the blockage causes. We do this by rating the intensity of the block using the SUDS scale (Subjective Units of Distress Scale), rated 10 to 0, where 10 is the worst it can be, and zero means it's not there. Testing on this scale is important so you can check what progress is being made in clearing the blockage. This is also important because if a block, either physical or emotional, goes away quickly, we often forget how bad it was. We sometimes forget that we had it at all. With the SUDS scale, you are reminded of where you started.

The VOC scale: Validity of Cognition. This scale is used to test for beliefs or how true one believes something to be. When used in clinical physiology, the VOC scale has only seven subdivisions between completely true and untrue. We are using ten in this book for simplicity. How true is this for you?

If you can't muscle test (as explained in Chapter Five), you may chose this method to test instead.

Removing the Blocks in Your Way

Step three is a simple action using the thymus/heart chakra that you can do to help you let go of the feeling or beliefs you are currently identifying. Place your hand on your thymus point; take a deep breath in, hold it to the count of seven, then let go. Identify this feeling. Were you able to reach a momentary point of well-being or peace?

There are many reasons why I have chosen the thymus/heart position in the Balance Procedure:

- In traditional Tibetan teaching, the thymus/heart chakra share the same energy.

- The thymus/heart chakra links our physical and non-physical aspects.

105

- This chakra is the centre of love, harmony, and balance.

- The thymus gland is important because it is the physical centre of immunity in the body.

- This point also anchors intention.

- Messages pass from the thymus to the brain and vice versa.

- A major discovery of behavioural kinesiology is that the thymus gland monitors and regulates energy flow in the meridian system.

The fourth step is identifying your balanced and harmonious state in your natural being. How does it feel when you are centred? Do any of these adjectives fit: calm, focused, energised, committed, peaceful, vital, effortless, confident, or satisfied?

The fifth step is to check how you feel. When you're not neutral, are you feeling panicky? Use your level from either the SUDS scale or the VOC scale, or muscle test to find if there is any discomfort. If you have anything remaining, it doesn't mean that the Balance Procedure hasn't worked; it just means there's some more work to be done to release the block totally, once and for all.

Scan your body to see if you have any other discomfort. How do you feel? Is there any remaining block or belief? If there is, measure the level either with the SUD or VOC scale or with muscle testing. Return to the action of breathing in to the count of seven and letting it go while your hand is over your thymus point/heart chakra. Remember, thoughts, feelings, and emotions are all energy, so when we change what we're thinking and feeling, the energy within us *literally shifts*. It changes into a different flow and causes different sensations. Seek out and hold on to the good, uplifting, and peaceful feelings.

The seventh step is to express gratitude. The expression of gratitude comes from the heart and should be "heartfelt." I'd like to share this beautiful poem with you about gratitude.

BE THANKFUL

*Be thankful that you don't already have
everything you desire,
If you did, what would there be to look
forward to?*

*Be thankful when you don't know
something
For it gives you the opportunity to learn.*

*Be thankful for the difficult times.
During those times you grow.*

*Be thankful for your limitations
Because they give you opportunities for
improvement.*

*Be thankful for each new challenge
Because it will build your strength
and character.*

*Be thankful for your mistakes.
They will teach you valuable lessons.*

*Be thankful when you're tired and weary
Because it means you've made a difference.*

*It is easy to be thankful for the good things.
A life of rich fulfillment comes to those
who are also thankful for the setbacks.*

JENNY COX

GRATITUDE can turn a negative
into a positive.
Find a way to be thankful for your troubles
and they can become your blessings.

– Author Unknown
(http://colleenscorner.com/Gratitude.html)

The entry for "Gratitude" on Wikipedia, an online encyclopaedia, tells us of its health benefits:

Research has suggested that feelings of gratitude may be beneficial to subjective emotional well-being (Emmons & McCullough, 2003). For example, Watkins and colleagues (Watkins et al., 2003) had participants test a number of different gratitude exercises, such as thinking about a living person for whom they were grateful, writing about someone for whom they were grateful, and writing a letter to deliver to someone for whom they were grateful. Participants in the control condition were asked to describe their living room. Participants who engaged in a gratitude exercise showed increases in their experiences of positive emotion immediately after the exercise, and this effect was strongest for participants who were asked to think about a person for whom they were grateful. Participants who had grateful personalities to begin with showed the greatest benefit from these gratitude exercises. In people who are grateful in general, life events have little influence on experienced gratitude (McCullough, Tsang & Emmons, 2004).

(http://en.wikipedia.org/wiki/Gratitude)

The more you do this procedure, the easier it becomes, and the quicker and more permanently you can let go of each blockage you identify. Your belief system is the foundation from which all your thoughts, feelings, and actions stem.

Now that you've identified who you want to be and what you want to do and have, let's look at the blocks you perceive to be in your way of accomplishing those things. They may *appear* as if the blocks are real, tangible things (time, availability, money, ability), but in reality most of the blocks are an issue of perception and belief. Nine times out of 10 the blockage has to do with fear and anxiety. Where there's fear and anxiety, there's stagnation. Somehow, when you transform your beliefs, what was once a block becomes doable. New beliefs can allow you to see your way around or through the blocks.

Changing Your Beliefs 109

So far this book has mainly engaged you at the reading level. Changing the beliefs that are causing you pain is where "the rubber really hits the road." If you are serious about wanting to turn your life around, then you're going to have to go beyond simply reading. You will not experience any lasting change reading about ideas. Oh, I'm all for ideas. I love to read, too. But real change doesn't happen until it's personal. And it requires action.

I don't know if you're like me, but I have read a lot of books, attended a lot of programs, listened to countless tapes, and talked about personal growth an awful lot. But none of this made a huge difference in how I felt, what I did, or what I received, at least not long-term. Change comes with taking action. We must face the fears and anxieties and learn to let them go. It happens too often that well-meaning individuals make glib statements like, "Just let it go," referring to fears, dilemmas, and perceived injuries. But what does that mean? How does one "just let it go?" How do we move past these obstacles into the life for which we long?

If you see a difference between where you are and where you want to be, consciously change your thoughts, words, and actions to match your grandest vision. This might require tremendous mental and physical effort. It will entail constant, moment-to-moment monitoring of your every thought, word, and deed. It will involve continued choice-making on a conscious level. This whole process is a massive move toward consciousness.

What you will find out if you undertake this challenge is that you've spent half your life unconscious. Isn't that scary? That is to say, you have been unaware, on a conscious level, of what you are choosing in the way of thoughts, words, and deeds until you experience the aftermath of them. Then, when you experience these results, you deny that your thoughts, words, and deeds had anything to do with them. We often see the aftermath of our choices as things that were done to us, bad luck, or other power-draining blaming patterns. Many of us have refused to take responsibility for the life we have *because of our choices.* As I've mentioned earlier, in the words of Lisa Nichols, "What we think about we bring about."

I'm telling you this because I've been where you are. If you're reading this, you're searching for answers. Although the Balance Procedure has been compared to many different types of psychotherapies, it is radically different than anything I've ever experienced. It's the only process I've found that not only helped me change my mind, but also produced visible differences in my life. And isn't that what we all want? It's nice to feel inspired and to get high off a new realisation, but what I really wanted was to feel better about myself and my life on a more confident and continual basis. I wanted to be able to pursue my desires without all the fears that tugged at me constantly. And those fears were numerous. I wanted to make more lasting changes where I didn't keep falling back into old habits that weren't working. The Balance Procedure did all that for me.

Beliefs

Beliefs are any ideas you think are true about yourself, others and life. Many of the beliefs you hold today are the result of (a) what your parents or guardians believed and passed along to you in the form of "gospel truth," (b) suggestions that you accepted as truth because of their role in your life, (c) what your friends believed, and (d) what you've been told is true by any authority whom you perceive to be credible. Beliefs may be religious or spiritual in nature, or they may reflect how you feel about your abilities. For example, if you were told that you are an idiot, even if the speaker was joking, you may have imposed great limitations on your intellectual capacities. If only on a subconscious level, you took on the belief that you are not intelligent.

111

You may have established ideas or beliefs about what is possible in your financial world because, for example, you may have been told, "You have to work long, hard hours for money," or, "You can't make any money in that field," or even, "Rich people are all crooks."

Examine the beliefs you have about all areas of life. Do you think that perfection was limited to only the chosen few? Do you think "God" has favourites? (There are over six billion people in this world, and each person has his or her own thoughts about God. Use what suits you.) Being separated from God is the very notion of "hell" for some religions. We've often been taught contradictory things about the nature of God. "He" is a wrathful, jealous god, or "He" is a kind and loving father. I can point you to the one that will make you feel more at peace if this is your concept of God. On an energetic level, if you choose to see the Almighty Creative Force as an anthropomorphic angry figure, what is produced in your life? Suffering. If you see Him (or Her or It) as a loving, benevolent form that wants you to experience a joyous life, what will then result? Joy. Even our thoughts on God and spirituality are all energy. You need not give up your religious faith in order to use these practices. If you see God as a loving Father who sent His son, Jesus, to lead you, then use Jesus' example of perfection to restore you to balance.

If you think Buddha was "right on," use his ideas on peace and "right thought" to help dispel any old beliefs that do not serve your human form. Each faith teaches that life is a gift to be enjoyed. Take care of the "temple," and start by guiding your thoughts and deeds toward those that make you feel good. Even the "Oracle at Delphi," an ancient Greek source for truth and wisdom, said, "Know thyself." Well-being and peace is the real message of all spirituality. When we work toward our own well-being, then we have the energy to help others find the same.

Are You Anxious?

How many people have you met just this past week that have mentioned that they "suffer from stress or anxiety?" It isn't even considered rare anymore, and allopathic doctors are quite often prescribing anti-anxiety medications for anyone who shows a symptom of it. MOST of the anxiety remedies from the Western pharmaceutical industry have adverse side-effects, such as drowsiness and the possibility of suicidal tendencies. This warning alone should be enough to make any informed individual reject such medications, but we don't. We have been conditioned to believe that any remedy must have "side effects" and that medication defeats discomfort. Is wishing for death as a solution to one's life preferable to anxiety? That is ridiculous.

THE BALANCE PROCEDURE

Let's look at it this way: Anxiety is a form of fear that happens as a result of thoughts, rather than because of real and imminent danger. The adrenaline has built up and up — causing more thoughts, which in turn trigger more adrenaline release. There are many symptoms associated with anxiety: anxiety attacks, panic attacks, anxiety disorders, stress disorders, sleep disorders, and depression. Because each person has a unique chemical make-up, the symptoms and their intensity will vary from person to person. Our society and the way we live is full of stresses; we know just about everyone is "stressed out" most of the time.

These are some of the more common anxiety symptoms that can affect the mind, body, and spirit of a person. This list isn't exhaustive.

- Clumsiness

- Disorientation

- Falling sensation

- Flu-like symptoms

- General malaise

- Hyperactivity, excess energy, nervous energy

- Increased or decreased sex drive

- Muscle twitching

- Neck, back, or shoulder pain, tightness or stiffness

- Night sweats

- Feeling lethargic or tired

- Easily startled

- Weight loss or gain

- Frequent yawning to try and catch your breath

- A heightened fear of what people think of you

- Fear of being trapped in a place with no exits

- Constant feeling of being overwhelmed

- Fear of being in public

- Fear of making mistakes or making a fool of yourself to others

- Fear of passing out

- Fears about irrational things, objects, circumstances, or situations

- Heightened self-awareness or self-consciousness

- Frequent headaches, migraine headaches

- Clenching of the jaw or grinding of the teeth

- Ringing in the ears, noises in the ears, noises in the head

- Fear of everything

- Desensitization

- Difficulty concentrating, thinking, speaking, forming thoughts, or following conversations

THE BALANCE PROCEDURE

- Fear of going crazy

- Repetitive thinking or incessant "mind chatter"

- Feeling that you are carrying the world on your shoulders

- Always feeling angry

- Lack of patience

- Depression

- Emotions that feel wrong

- Feeling down in the dumps

- Frequently being on edge or grouchy

- Frequently feel like crying for no apparent reason

- Having no feelings about things you used to

- Not feeling like yourself, detached from loved ones, emotionally numb

- Underlying anxiety, apprehension, or fear

- Constant craving for sugar or sweets

- Difficulty swallowing

- Skin problems, infections, or rashes

- Burning skin sensations, skin sensitivity

- Difficulty falling or staying asleep

- **Insomnia or waking up ill in the middle of the night**

- **Jolting awake**

- **Waking up in a panic attack**

- **Distorted, foggy, or blurred vision**

- **Dry, watery, or itchy eyes**

- **Eyes sensitive to light**

- **Depth perception that feels wrong**

As we dwell on past events or imagine future ones in our highly developed forebrains, our bodies circulate stress bio chemicals. So instead of the short-lived "fight-or-flight" response necessary for the present, the reaction persists over very long periods. One of the symptoms of stress disorders is insomnia. Sleep is very important for our immune system. With our busy lives, many of us just don't get enough sleep. Our bodies do all kinds of important healing when we are sleeping. Hormones and chemicals are released during sleep cycles that aren't produced during any other time. Insulin, which helps us process energy, is often lacking in people who are deprived of sleep.

Our natural defence cells, which fight against infections, cancer, and other diseases, don't function well when we are sleep-deprived. We must calm ourselves down immediately using the Balance Procedure, so we can get proper sleep, eat properly, feel strong and healthy, and handle anything that comes our way. The learned ability to "go with the flow" restores our balance, allowing us to eliminate the blockages and create the life of health and wealth we strive for.

When our energy system runs calmly and clearly, our thoughts can't help but run calmly and clearly as well. Energy, body, and thought are one and the same, and the state of one reflects the state of the other. Your active contribution to your well-being, life, and goals (or wildest dreams) is to want to do this process and to want to continue to prepare yourself to embrace each day as the gift it is intended to be.

Summary of the Balance Procedure

How does it work with the spirit, mind, and body?

Spirit: By placing your hands on your heart/thymus you are balancing your energy between the physical and spiritual aspects of your being – centring your energies.

Mind: Placing both hands on your thymus brings your left and right brain hemispheres together, completing the circuit that allows left–right integration of your goal.

Body: The hand placed on the heart/thymus is naturalistic. You will often see people holding their chest when placed in a situation of shock, trauma, or hysterical laughter; it is a way of centring naturally.

CHAPTER SEVEN

Keeping the Balance

119

BALANCE PROCEDURE

What do I want?

Block/Belief What is stopping me from having it	Apprehension How do I feel? What is my emotion?	Level Where are you NOW?	ACTION Thymus Heart Point	Natural calm, relaxed	Check Feeling emotion Scan your body	Express Gratitude

The diagram above is a tool to help you see, literally visualise in diagram form, how the Balance Procedure can transform you. It does this because you make the effort and change your habits, tendencies, and reactions to the stresses around you. As I've said earlier, the most important energy point on the human body is the thymus point, or heart chakra. This is the energy reactor at the centre of the energy system. It powers the entire energy system and is intrinsically linked to every part of us: thought, physical body parts, or meridians.

When you are able to get the thymus point stabilised, all of your systems will be stronger, more powerful, and work better. It really is that simple to restore balance in your life. As our central stabilizer, it is important to do this process at least three times per day.

THE BALANCE PROCEDURE

Place both hands on the centre of your chest and close your eyes. Take a deep breath in and let it out for a count of seven. Open your eyes and say, "BALANCE." Are you in harmony? Do you have a new awareness? Do you feel comfortable, optimistic, and confident? Have you reached your natural state, your state of equilibrium? If not, repeat as necessary. You'll find the more often you do it, the less often it becomes necessary to do it. But we must remember that each new day brings new challenges, and we can meet these obstacles and blocks with ease if we are *already* balanced. Do this regularly and you will find that it becomes easier to slow down and to calm down when the unexpected arises. You'll more easily create those periods of peace and joy when you can handle things without upset.

You can also use your meridian tapping points under the eye, switching from side to side as you think or say, "Adrenalin allergy." Do this until you can make a sigh of relief, which is a sign that the tension and adrenalin are receding.

I've had some amazing feedback and experiences with this process. I've included only a few, though the responses are pouring in daily. Here is one of my favourites. The following is an example of the Balance Procedure being used in practice in a very real and practical way — the labour and delivery process of childbirth. Explained in the words of therapist Melanie Wright, this is the explanation of how the Balance Procedure was used during labour for pain relief and contraction regulation.

My sister Amy started having regular complementary therapy treatments as soon as she announced she was expecting and had reflexology and Reiki throughout her pregnancy. When she was in the latter stages of pregnancy, she was experiencing pelvic discomfort, and she found that EFT was really effective for pain relief.

Toward the end of her pregnancy, I attended an introductory course in Balance with Jenny in Cambridge. I was so enthused with it that I suggested to Amy that we should try Balance for pain relief, which she agreed sounded like a good idea.

When Amy's water broke late on a Sunday night, the contractions progressed, and Amy and her partner went into the local maternity hospital. The midwives advised Amy to rest at home because the contractions weren't regular enough, and she should report to hospital on Tuesday if things hadn't progressed sooner than that.

Amy let me know that she had returned home on Monday, and I suggested that I go round to see if I could help with pain relief, which she thought was a good idea. When I got to her home, I found that the contractions were continuing but weren't getting any stronger or more regular. Amy had already used Reiki (she is attuned to second-degree level) and EFT ever since her waters had broken on Sunday, and had found that they had helped with keeping herself calm.

On Monday evening, we used Reiki to help pick up Amy's energy and reflexology to help the contractions progress. When doing the Reiki, we found there was a natural pattern to the contractions. First, I would find that the baby's energy levels would increase significantly, becoming evident by a tingling sensation rising up my arms to my elbows, then followed by me suddenly getting a "head rush," even though I had grounded myself well before the treatment. The baby would then wriggle, and Amy would feel her temperature rise.

Approximately two minutes after this, the contraction would happen.

After spending some time doing these treatments to help increase her energy, Amy decided that she would like a bath and an early night, so I went home and instructed her to call me if she needed me.

I called her again on Tuesday morning to see how the night had progressed. Amy said the contractions were still happening, but had lost any kind of regular pattern and were now only every 20, 25, or 30 minutes. (Anyone who has ever experienced labour knows that failure to progress is not only dangerous, it is exhausting for the mother who needs strength for the birth process.)

I went to visit her on Tuesday to see if I could assist in any way, and when I got there we remembered our earlier conversation about the Balance Procedure. We decided to give it a try. When I first arrived, the contractions had been very irregular, and we decided to use Balance to see if we could make them more regular.

Amy applied the Balance Procedure and set her intention on the contractions being regular and every 12 minutes. Because of the experience the night before, we knew the pattern with the contractions, and I tuned into both Amy's and the baby's energies and was able to say when a contraction was on the way. Once Amy noticed her temperature rising, she applied Balance once again but this time for pain relief.

To our amazement, when we looked at the clock the contraction had arrived bang on 12 minutes, despite the contractions being very irregular and the previous one being about 30 minutes apart from the one before that!

Very impressed with the results, we decided to do it again, so Amy put her intention on wanting the next contraction to be in 12 minutes time. Right on cue, at 12 minutes, the next contraction arrived. We were excited by this and decided to see whether the previous two contractions had been a fluke and did Balance once again for a 12-minute interval. Again, you could have set your watch by it!

We now decided to experiment, and Amy applied The Balance Procedure to make the gap 10 minutes. Time after time, the contractions were spot on, so we reduced the time span to eight minutes, then seven.

Amy had also been applying Balance for pain relief during the contractions. After the contractions Amy would open one eye, look at me and say, "Well, I think that was a contraction but it didn't hurt." Although Amy could feel her stomach tightening during the contractions, the Balance Procedure worked effectively for pain relief.

In the lead up to one of the contractions, Amy decided that she wouldn't use the Balance Procedure for pain relief to just check whether she was actually having full contractions, owing to her lack of any real pain. So as the contraction approached, Amy didn't apply the technique and went through the contraction without any form of pain relief.

This contraction was significantly stronger and a lot more uncomfortable. After the contraction, Amy opened her eyes, looked at me, and said, "Balance is definitely the way to go. I'm not doing that again without Balance!"

Amy had made contact with the maternity hospital during one of her breaks from contractions, and went into the hospital to have her baby, still applying Balance for pain relief all the way.

Baby Miles Horwood is the first baby in the world to have his mum apply the Balance Procedure for pain relief during labour, and judging by the results, he certainly isn't going to be the last!

I'm very proud to have been the very first therapist in the world to have been able to assist a mother in her pain relief during labour using the Balance Procedure.

THE BALANCE PROCEDURE

In her own words, Amy said, "I would definitely recommend anyone using the Balance Procedure for pain relief, because I found it very effective and calming, and I would definitely use it for the same situation again – although I'm not planning that for some time!"

Now that I know how Balance works, how effective it is, and also how simple it is to use, I know I would use it for any situation or pain relief that I need in the future.

A complementary therapist for more than seven years, Melanie is also a Meridian Energy therapist. A fellow of the International Council of Holistic Therapists and a member of the Association for the Advancement of Meridian Energy Therapies, Melanie has her own practice and is a motivational speaker.

This firsthand testimony is very exciting. The idea can easily be adjusted for a variety of situations involving issues of pain. Perhaps you fear the dentist, yet you want to avoid painful, risky sedation and shots. Why not try the Balance Procedure? Or perhaps you have experienced some traumatic injury or broken bone. The technique is easily used to relieve pain from all sorts of discomfort.

Let's put this into action. Pick one of your anxieties.

- **Is it a limiting belief?**

- **Is it a feeling of anxiety?**

- **Where is it?**

- **How does it feel?**

- **Does it have a colour?**

- **Does it have a shape?**

Identify it and assign it a rating on the Subjective Units of Distress Scale that we discussed earlier. There is another worksheet at the end of this chapter for just this purpose. What is its value on the scale? It helps to be able to look at the belief you have about your anxiety on paper, because then you can see and rate how it affects you overall.

Now let's take ACTION WITH INTENTION.

- **Place your hand on the thymus point.**

- **Breathe in for a count of seven.**

- **Hold for a count of seven.**

- **As you breathe out say, "Balance."**

Have you achieved the desired state of "neutral?" What does neutral feel like? Identify that and remember it. It is what you will continue to aim for each day that you do this in order to transform your life. Check for other anxieties you may be affected by in the moment by holding the thymus point again and mentally scanning your body. If there is any tension, then repeat the Balance Procedure and let go.

This is all you need for a quick anxiety stopper, especially if you are short of time or dealing with a child or friend with anxiety. See what being in neutral feels like. If you feel you have any lingering anxiety, then go to "check."

Check

What is your level now?

- SUDS: Compare these next two to the value you assigned to them earlier.

- VOCs

- How do you feel?

- Are you relaxed?

- Is this how you would like to feel?

- Go inside yourself. If you have any anxiety or pain remaining, go back to your level stage and repeat the process.

127

Your aim is to be completely free of the anxiety when the block has disappeared or has been transformed into something positive and productive. Your life-energy has been stimulated. Enjoy the moment; allow the feeling to expand. Feel your soul begin to expand. Feel your uniqueness; hold the awareness that only you are here and now in this space and time.

When all is complete, be sure to express gratitude. The thymus point is the dual-hemisphere, creative approach to the blocks. This instantly transforms the negative emotion into a positive one.

The Balance Procedure is not limited to the removal of pain, but it can be life-saving, as you'll see in the following information. It involves my very own wonderful husband, Alan. During a recent trip to Anglia University, we did a quick experiment with the psychology department's equipment, which monitored his stress levels and heart rate. We only had time to do one experiment using the Balance Procedure.

Alan was hooked up to the equipment, and he was asked to think of a situation that caused him stress. He focused on a speech that he was doing the next day, and his heartbeat went to over 100 beats per minute! His normal rate was a healthy 82, which went down dramatically to 64. This also shows how detrimental prolonged stress is to our physical well-being. Just thinking about something stressful can raise one's heart rate in an instant. Using the Balance Procedure, Alan's heart rate immediately went down to 58. It transformed the fear into positive, productive energy that he was able to use the next day. We are planning more experiments with similar equipment.

The Importance of the Number Seven

I'd like to comment here on the number seven. I decided early on while writing this book that I wanted to present it in seven chapters because the number seven comes up so often. Even this week I was in a workshop learning how to make the classical seven-circuit labyrinth in my garden. The symbol of a labyrinth is very old and well-known in many cultures. Probably the most popular historic representations of a labyrinth are Mandela (a metaphysical pattern of cosmos in Hinduism and Buddhism) and the Minotaur Labyrinth in Greek mythology. These are meditation tools, patterns designed for you to take your focus away from your everyday thoughts. A labyrinth in a garden is designed to be walked while meditating. You are never sure where you go next (unless you know the pattern well), and you learn to trust the process and therefore your own progress.

- I feel that there is something very special about the number seven.

- When people are asked to choose their lucky number, most people opt for seven.

- We have seven days of the week, and there are seven ages of man.

- God rested on the seventh day after creating the world.

129

- Every cell in the human body is renewed in seven years! We're literally new every seven years.

- In ancient cosmology, the seven planetary spheres encompassed the Earth.

- There are seven pillars of wisdom.

- There are seven deadly sins, and there are seven main chakras.

- There are seven colours in the visible light spectrum or rainbow, and when these colour rays are refocused through a prism, they magically re-combine into white light. A group of seven therefore can have the hidden meaning of being separate colours or frequencies that go together to make the one or wholeness.

There's a lovely experiment on the site below regarding Sir Isaac Newton's Prism Experiment (http://micro.magnet.fsu.edu/ primer/java/scienceopticsu/newton/). It tells us:

> In 1665, Isaac Newton was a young scientist studying at Cambridge University in England. He was very interested in learning all about light and colours. One bright sunny day, Newton darkened his room and made a hole in his window shutter, allowing just one beam of sunlight to enter the room. He then took a glass prism and placed it in the sunbeam. The result was a spectacular multicoloured band of light just like a rainbow. The multicoloured band of light is called a colour spectrum.
>
> Newton believed that all the colours he saw were in the sunlight shining into his room. He thought he then should be able to combine the colours of the spectrum and make the light white again. To test this, he placed another prism upside-down in front of the first prism. He was right. The band of colours combined again into white sunlight. Newton was the first to prove that white light is made up of all the colours that we can see.

Newton's discovery is directly related to the Balance Procedure. I've exposed you to my discovery about the simplicity of restoring your body to "neutral" via certain channels of energy called chakras. Each chakra contains a colour. Colours are particles of light that together make up a whole. The colours of the rainbow expose us to nature's perfection and natural ability to balance. It is a glimpse of the divine. In the Jewish TaNak, or Christian Old Testament, God revealed a rainbow as a sign of His covenant. We have the ability to tap into this source of light, energy, and perfection in order to flood it into our own physical and emotional bodies, filling us with radiant perfection. We find the heart chakra. We breathe in to the count of seven. We identify neutral. We hold for seven. To me, seven is a perfect number for many beautiful reasons.

CONCLUSION:

What the Balance Procedure Can Do For You and Those Around You

131

THE BALANCE PROCEDURE

- Can help change your mind, where you can visibly see the differences in your life.

- Can help you feel inspired.

- Can help you more consistently feel better about yourself and your life.

- Can help you pursue your desires without distress.

- Can help make more permanent changes, preventing you from falling back into old habits.

The Balance Procedure helps you to do all of this for yourself and for others.

- Awareness is the first step in the Balance Procedure.

- As you grow in self-awareness, you will better understand why you feel what you feel and why you behave as you behave.

- That understanding then gives you the opportunity and freedom to change those things you'd like to change about yourself and create the life you want.

- Without knowing who you are, self-acceptance and change become impossible.

132

Everyone was born with an intention to create through thought and imagination. The Balance Procedure is a series of carefully designed questions and actions that help you identify and change (if you wish) those beliefs that are causing your pain, fear, anxiety, anger, or depression, freeing you from the limitations we place on *ourselves and others*. The Balance Procedure is designed to transform you and those with whom you share it.

Awareness of our tendencies allows us to recognise that we have a block that it is hurting us and others. Then you can do the Balance Procedure with conviction. You will be activating your will to be well and happy, and you will overcome the blocks with a positive feeling.

The wonderful thing about the Balance Procedure is that it works on the root cause of our imbalances. It transforms the blocks and obstacles so that the block no longer exists; it has been turned into something positive, productive, and life-affirming, and your life-energy has been stimulated. This instantly transforms negative emotions into positive ones. Wanting to do this process and continue to do it is your active contribution to your well-being, your life, and your goal.

In Chapter Seven, we showed a good example of using the Balance Procedure with physical pain experienced during childbirth. Many of you are probably wondering how to remedy areas of your life that may not be related to physical pain. Our discomfort with finances can cause distress in what should be a life of happiness and love. Can we use this fantastic technique to help us in this area? Absolutely! Once again, therapist Melanie Wright would like to share her personal story on this subject.

An example of how the Balance Procedure can have a positive and immediate effect is documented by Melanie when she applied the procedure. Melanie explains:

> I attended an introductory course on the Balance Procedure with Jenny in Cambridge. As part of the course, we had to pick an area of life that we wanted to improve upon. Like most therapists, and indeed most people, I have an issue with my relationship with money. My main issue is that I feel insecure about having enough money – something which I am working on!
>
> Jenny explained that often our fear of not having enough money comes down to not feeling secure and a lack of trust in our financial safety. Working with Balance, I broke this issue down and came up with a statement of intent that, "I always have more than enough money for what I need and want."
>
> The workshop finished on Sunday afternoon, and I headed off home feeling very enthused, excited, and yet very

calm and peaceful. What I observed over the next 24 hours was nothing short of incredible. By Monday evening I had secured almost £500 of extra, unexpected income!

One place I worked at asked me on Monday morning to do some extra work for them. I sent an invoice to another practice where I worked, and had remembered to include something on the invoice that I had forgotten about previously. Somebody else called on the off-chance and asked me to do some work for them as a matter of urgency, and I received calls from clients wanting unexpected treatments.

All this had come about through focusing on those behaviour thoughts and patterns that were not serving me and switching my focus onto those that which I did wish for myself.

134

Balance is quick, easy, simple, and yet very effective – in short, an amazing therapy which is going to take therapists and the world by storm!

Sometimes we create stresses on ourselves, especially in relationship to money, the lack thereof, and the fear of what it means to not have enough. By balancing ourselves and opening up these channels, we not only bring physical peace upon our bodies, but we also open ourselves up to the abundance that we deserve. Stressing out about money shuts down our immune system and changes our overall participation in the world. As we can see from Melanie's story, she was balanced and therefore open to receiving additional, *unexpected income*. She changed her "self-dialogue," and her situation improved immediately.

Although the process has been designed as a self-help tool, it is our intention to practice and train practitioners in the Balance Procedure so that people can really reap the full benefits and learn how to use the process. It will be easier for trained practitioners to share this information once they are certified and can instruct others in this practice. For those of you who would like to train or have the process as an add-on to the therapies that you are already doing, it will be more readily available as we continue to teach this in seminar form and for certification.

People often get stuck on their "self-dialogue." Old habits are often hard to break, but it is not impossible. It is very, very possible. It is our intention that, after one or two sessions with a Balance practitioner, people will find it much easier to "self-dialogue."

When I first did the process on my own, I kept getting stuck. After working with Alan and a few close friends, I was better able to do the dialogues by myself. Human interaction is important. We came into this world as groups. Sharing this information and all other things that are good is my mission. Even if you just pass along what helps you to others, you are performing a great deed, and the universe, God, or whatever you acknowledge as the guiding force of "energy" will respond in kind. But we do, as humans, need to share with others to help alleviate suffering. And this Balance Procedure is simple and non-invasive.

Remember to laugh. Find a group such as a laughter yoga community or another organisation to help you practice joy *and laughter* daily. For further information, visit www.laughteryoga.org. The breathing techniques of yoga have been proven beneficial in helping one maintain or even achieve good health. One can always improve the technique as you learn ways to improve all areas of life. Just start balancing and you will find your life magically transformed. You will have no choice but to include others, because laughter is the best contagious thing I can think of to be exposed to regularly.

JENNY COX

One of the most fundamental basics of the Balance Procedure is taking 100% responsibility for everything we have created in our lives. Although some of our choices may be subconscious, by being accountable we empower ourselves with the ability to make different choices. The first step to make change is to focus very clearly on what you want, to make a very clear choice. We can begin to discover our deepest inner being, our true selves, and so to balance our energies to achieve our positive goals. You will know your purpose in life and can set about achieving it.

ABOUT THE AUTHOR

Jenny Cox is a Meridian Energy advanced practitioner/ trainer, an NLP Practitioner, a practitioner and trainer in holistic therapies, and a Reiki master. As a certified teacher, Jenny won the National Regional New Horizons Award in 2005 for her teaching in Cambridge, United Kingdom.

For the past 20 years, Jenny has used many therapies and counselling methods in order to help her clients and herself find relief from physical and emotional discomforts. In 2003 Jenny was introduced to Meridian Energy Therapies, and became a practitioner and trainer in techniques, such as Emotional Freedom Technique (EFT) developed by Gary Craig, Be Set Free Fast developed by Larry Nims, and Tapas Acupressure Technique developed by Tapas Fleming, among others. From this base and the understanding of the aura, the meridian system, the chakras, and how they all interact, she was able to develop a technique called the Balance Procedure, which simplifies working with one's own energy to restore balance and harmony in order to promote health and overall well-being. She also incorporates colour, sound, and aromatherapy in her practice and teaching.

Jenny lives in Cambridge, United Kingdom, with her husband, Alan. They have two adult children, Sarah and Edward.

REFERENCES

www.aamet.org.

www.about.com.

Atkinson, William Walker. *Thought Vibration or the Law of Attraction in the Thought World*, 1906.

Bandura, Albert. *Adolescent Aggression*, 1959.

Bertalanffy, Karl Ludwig von. *General System Theory: Foundations, Development,*

Applications, New York, 1968.

Boeree, Dr. C. George. "Albert Bandura." 2006.

Brodie, Renee. *Let Light into Your Heart with Colour and Sound*, 2001.

Byrne, Rhonda and Bob Proctor, et al. DVD *The Secret.*

Callaghan, Dr. Roger. Thought Field Therapy (TFT).

www.chakra.com.

http://colleenscorner.com/Gratitude.html/

Craig, Gary. Freedom Technique (EFT).

Diamond, Dr. John. *Your Body Doesn't Lie,* 1989, and *Life Energy: Using the Meridians to Unlock the Hidden Power of Your Emotions,* 1992.

Einstein, Albert. "What Life Means to Einstein," *The Saturday Evening Post,* 1929 October 26.

www.emofree.com.

Fleming, Tapas. Tapas Acupressure Technique.

Gerber, Richard. *Vibrational Medicine,* 1996.

Gimbel, Theo. *Healing with Colour and Light,* 1994.

Gray, John. *Men are from Mars, Women are from Venus,* 1992.

Hougham, Paul. The Atlas Mind Body and Spirit.

www.kheper.net.

www.laughteryoga.org.

McGuinness, Helen. Holistic Therapies.

http://micro.magnet.fsu.edu/primer/java/scienceopticsu/newton/.

Nims, Larry, Ph.D. and Joan Sotkin. *Be Set Free Fast,* (BSFF), 1997.

Rosenberg, Marshall B. *Nonviolent Communication: A Language of Compassion,* 1999.

http://theamt.com.

Wattles, Wallace D. *The Science of Getting Rich,* 1910.

http://webspace.ship.edu/cgoboer/bandura.html.

http://en.wikipedia.org/wiki/Gratitude.

THE ASSOCIATION FOR THE ADVANCEMENT OF MERIDIAN ENERGY THERAPIES (AAMET)

A non-profit making organisation open to all

Meridian Energy Therapies are causing a transformation in complimentary medicine, as we know it.
Find out more by visiting www.aamet.org

- **Find a certified AAMET Meridian Therapist near you**
- **Download free materials**
- **Free e-mail group for discussions – open to all**
- **Book Reviews**
- **Latest News and up-to-dates**
- **Interesting Articles written by Experts in the Advancement of Meridian Energy Therapies**
- **Case Studies**
- **Latest techniques developed in Meridian Energy Therapy**
- **National and International listings of training workshops**
- **There is something for everyone**

These are exciting times for all!

Federation of Holistic Therapists
The UK's largest professional therapist association

FHT

The Federation of Holistic Therapists (FHT) is the *largest membership* association in the UK, representing over 20,000 beauty, complementary and sports therapists.

Established in 1962, the FHT is an independent, *not-for-profit* association that has been advocating *high professional standards* for over 40 years. All members are required to abide by the FHT Code of Ethics and Professional Practice, thus safeguarding the health and safety of the public and the reputation of the industry as a whole.

The FHT offers its members a wide range of benefits, including

- an annual subscription to International Therapist magazine, published six times a year

- access to great value public liability insurance cover (up to £6m)

- active campaigning by FHT to promote and protect your interests as a practising therapist

- a unique lapel badge, membership card and certificate of professional membership

- access to our website, where you can chat to other therapists, update your details on our 'Find a therapist' online register and read over 150 therapy-related articles

- an FHT Members' Catalogue, offering over 700 quality therapy products from one convenient source

- a comprehensive education programme, with concessionary rates for members

- business and therapy advice from the FHT help line

- support from one of over 65 FHT Local Support Groups

For more information: 0870 420 2022 • www.fht.org.uk • info@fht.org.uk

Feel the benefit...

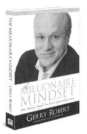

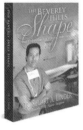
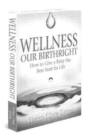

OTHER BOOKS FROM LIFESUCCESS PUBLISHING

 Stop Singing The Blues
10 Powerful Strategies For Hitting The High Notes In Your Life

Dr. Cynthia Barnett
ISBN # 978-1-59930-022-1

 Don't Be A Victim,
Protect Yourself
Everything Seniors Need To Know To Avoid Being Taken Financially

Jean Ann Dorrell
ISBN # 978-1-59930-024-5

 A "Hand Up", not a "Hand Out"
The best ways to help others help themselves

David Butler
ISBN # 978-1-59930-071-9

 Doctor Your Medicine Is Killing Me!
One Mans Journey From Near Death to Health and Wellness

Pete Coussa
ISBN # 978-1-59930-047-4

 I Believe in Me
7 Ways for Woman to Step Ahead in Confidence

Lisa Gorman
ISBN # 978-1-59930-069-6

 The Color of Success
Why Color Matters in your Life, your Love, your Lexus

Mary Ellen Lapp
ISBN # 978-1-59930-078-8

 If Not Now, When?
What's Your Dream?

Cindy Nielsen
ISBN # 978-1-59930-073-3

 The Skills to Pay the Bills… and then some!
How to inspire everyone in your organisation into high performance!

Buki Mosaku
ISBN # 978-1-59930-058-0